100 Things
I Learned
in
Heaven

An Extraordinary True Story of a Woman's
Battle with Darkness that Led Her to Journey
to Heaven Many Times.

Karen Bauer

BALBOA.
PRESS

A DIVISION OF HAY HOUSE

Balboa Press books may be ordered through booksellers or by contacting:

Balboa Press
A Division of Hay House
1663 Liberty Drive
Bloomington, IN 47403
www.balboapress.com
1 (877) 407-4847

Because of the dynamic nature of the Internet, any web addresses or links contained in this book may have changed since publication and may no longer be valid. The views expressed in this work are solely those of the author and do not necessarily reflect the views of the publisher, and the publisher hereby disclaims any responsibility for them.

The author of this book does not dispense medical advice or prescribe the use of any technique as a form of treatment for physical, emotional, or medical problems without the advice of a physician, either directly or indirectly. The intent of the author is only to offer information of a general nature to help you in your quest for emotional and spiritual well-being. In the event you use any of the information in this book for yourself, which is your constitutional right, the author and the publisher assume no responsibility for your actions.

Any people depicted in stock imagery provided by Thinkstock are models, and such images are being used for illustrative purposes only.
Certain stock imagery © Thinkstock.

Printed in the United States of America.

ISBN: 978-1-4525-2289-0 (sc)
ISBN: 978-1-4525-2291-3 (hc)
ISBN: 978-1-4525-2290-6 (e)

Library of Congress Control Number: 2014917271

Balboa Press rev. date: 11/7/2014

For Marie, you are the greatest gift
I have ever been given.
Your grace, beauty, and courage
continue to amaze me!

Contents

Introduction

I am just an ordinary girl from a farm in Iowa who has lived an extraordinary life. I recently moved back to the United States after twenty-two years of living abroad in Europe and Asia. I survived a long and fierce battle with darkness that led me into the light, where I learned and experienced much in heaven.

This battle with darkness began with a serious bacterial infection that developed during the birth of our daughter in Singapore in 1996. At this same time I felt that something evil had descended upon my husband, our baby daughter, and myself. Shortly after this I became ill and had a constant fever. I had numerous medical tests over several years, but none revealed a diagnosis. Many paranormal activities began to occur, and I felt as though this invisible enemy was threatening our lives. I kept praying and asking God to guide me and to show me who or what this invisible enemy was and how I could survive this battle.

In 2003, I had a traumatic brain injury and a severe concussion. Immediately following this blow to my head, I could temporarily see many things in the spiritual realms. It was similar to having a nightmare while being fully awake. When the darkness persisted and the symptoms and constant fever did not improve with any form of medical intervention, I did the only thing I knew to do. I clung to Jesus, and I prayed to all of heaven for help.

As a last resort, I sought the help of a spiritual healer and hypnotherapist from Hong Kong in 2004 while we were living in Shanghai. My sessions with her revealed that I had suffered a near-death experience when I was three years old and multiple severe head injuries when I was six years old. During these events the trauma was so severe that I disassociated from my body. All of these occurrences in my life led to my experiences in heaven and the discovery of my divine life mission and true soul purpose during this lifetime.

During my first meeting with the spiritual healer, Mabel, we were visited by a huge, powerful archangel. From this moment on my entire world was split open. I was living in the physical world but could now see into the spiritual realms. My entire life was then saturated with angelic visitations and highly spiritual experiences. My dreams, prayer time, meditation, hypnotherapy, and normal waking hours were filled with angels in many different forms. I continued to be taken to heaven for lessons and healing almost every week until August of 2005 and several more times in the subsequent years. After I was in heaven for the first time on November 27, 2004, I knew that I was changed forever.

I consider these journeys to heaven and angelic visitations to be the most extraordinary thing that any person could possibly experience while still on the earth. I felt incredibly honored and blessed. I understood that this was a gift and a privilege. I was very thankful, as I felt that everything I had learned in heaven and the healing I had received saved my life. However, to suddenly have my spiritual vision opened to everything in the spirit realms, including demons in many forms, people in heaven, and countless people who had died but had not yet gone to heaven, was for me extremely traumatic. I honestly do not think that I could have withstood being exposed to the dark entities and these other realms without constant help and comfort from the angels who never left my side. Furthermore, I had feared and avoided anything dark my entire life, so I was highly resistant to accepting this spiritual vision as a gift, and I wanted more than anything to just be *normal*.

My intention in briefly writing about the darkness I encountered is not to instill fear, shock anyone, or be controversial. I believe that each of us lives with some level of fear or darkness, or we know someone close to us who does. I feel that the power of the fear is removed when we understand the truth and it is demystified, and then healing may occur. What I learned in heaven is that the light and love of God are the most powerful tools and weapons in the entire universe and can easily conquer any fear or darkness. When we focus on the light and the love of God and use our authority as his child, our fear must diminish. My hope is that you are inspired to see that I am just a normal woman who survived this battle by asking heaven to intervene for me. And heaven responded in remarkable ways.

Everything I experienced in heaven was awe-inspiring. The most impressive thing of all was the incredible unconditional love of God and the indescribable joy that I felt every time I journeyed to and was in heaven. I wanted to tell the whole world about what I had experienced. I wished that I could climb to the top of the highest mountain and shout as loud as I possibly could to everyone that my voice could reach about how much God loved them unconditionally just as they are. I knew that this love and these messages I received in heaven belonged to all of mankind.

I longed to tell everyone I knew and loved about what I saw, felt, and experienced while I was in heaven. Although I realized that no human words could possibly come close to describing the overwhelming love, joy, peace, and acceptance that I felt every time I ascended to and was in heaven, I knew I needed to try.

Unfortunately, instead of climbing to the top of the highest mountain and telling the whole world about what I experienced in heaven, except for some of my immediate family members and a few close friends, I hid in my *spiritual closet* because of fear. I was afraid of people thinking I was crazy or misinterpreting my intentions, and I feared their criticism. Furthermore, I did not want to shame my husband, as he had a prominent position. I wondered how anyone could possibly believe or understand what I could not fully believe or understand myself. It has taken me several years to process all of this information. In addition, I am a fairly private person, and all of these experiences were very intimate. I knew that for me to tell my story in a way that would help others the most and at the same time completely convey all that I had learned while in heaven, I needed to reveal my authentic self and everything that I had undergone in my lifetime.

I can very much appreciate why many people may find it difficult to believe that I have been in heaven many times for learning and healing. If I had not lived through these experiences myself, I am certain I would be very skeptical as well. After all, I am not a priest, pastor, or saint. Nor am I perfect. I was broken and in great need of healing, and I continually cried out to God, Jesus, saints, and angels for help and guidance. And they answered in ways that I never could have imagined.

After God revealed to me what my soul purpose was, I asked God, "Why me?" I wondered if he had possibly gotten me mixed up with one of my siblings, as they are more intellectual and saintly and can even write beautifully. Some of them are so witty that they can make even the simplest story sound eloquent and very entertaining. He again took me to heaven and showed me exactly why this was my assignment. I was shown that I was asked to do a job before the time of my birth, and I agreed to do it. It was a sacred contract, and all of the events in my entire life were leading up to fulfilling this contract.

Because much of what I was taught in heaven was vastly different than what I had formerly believed and it was sometimes so far beyond my limited comprehension, I continued to be taken to heaven for further explanation and clarification until there was not a doubt in my mind about what God and the angels wanted me to understand and convey to the world. I believe I needed these lessons in heaven to increase my faith in God and in myself and to complete one of my main soul purposes, which I write about in this book. Now I know without a doubt that I am called to share what I learned and experienced while I was in heaven … and what I was repeatedly shown regarding the continuous cycle of life and death.

It was as though the lessons that I learned in heaven and what I saw, felt, and experienced in these other realms was imprinted upon my heart, mind, and soul forever. I knew that there were no books on the earth that could teach me what I learned from God and the angels.

Eventually I could not completely hide my authentic self anymore. Although I was trying very hard to keep all of this a secret, it seemed that I had an invisible sign on my forehead that said that I was "open for business." People I had never met before were drawn to me everywhere I went. I began teaching what I learned in heaven in our home in Germany. I also started using the gifts that I had acquired while in heaven to assist people in their own healing process. What I call "Love Letters from Heaven" began to flow through me. These were usually three pages of messages filled with love, hope, and inspiration from God, angels, guides, and loved ones who had passed on. After years of resistance I recognized this as a gift, and I realized that it is the most fulfilling work that I have ever done.

Now almost ten years after I was in heaven for the first time, I feel as big around as a Macy's Day Parade balloon that is about to burst if I do not finally share everything I learned in heaven and in the light in the form of this book. I no longer have a choice. I now realize that if I allow the fear of criticism to keep me silent, than I am choosing to make this about myself. When in reality, it is about the numerous life-changing truths that God and the angels revealed to me and asked me to share with as many people as I could.

I would prefer to entirely omit any mention of the darkness and the illness that I endured, but I recognize that it is also an important part of my journey, as it led me to what I learned while in heaven. I believe that without the help and intervention of angels and the teaching that I received in heaven during these darkest times, I would not be alive today.

Now I am passionately driven to share my experiences and these messages with anyone who is interested. I believe that even if someone has heard this information before or has read it in another's story of an experience in heaven, as long as I tell my own genuine story, even if it touches just one person and helps him or her to draw closer to God or to heal on his or her personal journey, then I have completed this assignment.

I was instructed that this first book and the messages it contains are to be presented as simply and straightforward as possible so that there is no mistake as to what I hope to communicate. I believe God often uses simple and imperfect people so there is no question that it is he who is working through them.

It was conveyed to me that these messages are for all people and that God loves us all the same. I believe that if everyone only knew how much love and help they have in heaven and how all of heaven is just waiting for us to ask for assistance and support in every situation, it would completely change their lives forever, and then they would be free to live their lives with increased hope, trust, power, and joy!

Just an Ordinary Girl

I am an ordinary girl from rural Iowa. I was born in 1964 and grew up on a big farm with my parents, four brothers, and four sisters. I am the eighth of nine children. Although we did not have many material possessions, I did not feel underprivileged. As we either raised or grew everything we needed ourselves, we were self-sufficient.

I loved growing up amid an abundance of nature and the freedom that the wide-open space provided. Having a large amount of land and many animals meant there was plenty of physical work to do, and all of us were expected to do our fair share. Summer days were especially filled with a variety of chores. We spent many hours walking up and down the mile-long soybean fields pulling and hoeing weeds, baling hay, picking up rocks, and gathering mustard. My father was ahead of his time in terms of conservation and did not believe in using chemicals on the land. This was a great thing, but it meant that there were many more weeds to pull than average. We learned to care for animals from an early age. We raised many cattle and pigs. In addition, two cows provided fresh milk, several chickens furnished eggs daily, and we enjoyed horses, rabbits, dogs, and cats as pets. During the winter months the boys continued with the outdoor chores with the livestock, and we girls mainly helped in the house.

Our large farmhouse was more than one hundred years old and was built by German settlers. We had a beautiful huge yard that was perfectly manicured. It resembled a park with many old trees and a wide variety of bushes and flowers. Both of my parents enjoyed gardening, and as there were many mouths to feed, our vegetable garden was substantial.

Every Saturday my mom baked fresh bread for the week and delicious cinnamon rolls for Sunday morning. While I worked regularly alongside her, I felt as though I was continuously learning, whether it was in the house or outside in the yard or garden. She taught me from an early age all of her domestic skills and at the same time expressed her thoughts and opinions about life, her faith, and the world almost constantly. From the time I can remember, she instilled confidence in me by expecting that I could successfully complete whatever task she asked of me. When it came to housework, homework, county fair entries, and science fair projects, she was quite competitive and often encouraged us with a great deal of praise for a job well done.

The closest town to our farm was Stacyville, which was five miles away. Stacyville had a population of 476 people. Almost everything in the community was centered around the church parish, and everyone, including many extended family members and all of our neighbors in the countryside, attended the same church. I treasure having been raised in such a wonderful community. Of anywhere I have traveled and lived in the world, the pure and genuine goodness, friendliness, and generous nature of the people in this community still impresses me to this day. I will always have many fond memories of my relatives and neighbors from my hometown.

Music was always a big part of our lives. Some of my best memories with my family and extended family on my mom's side involve singing together. My parents, siblings, aunts, uncles, and many cousins have been blessed with beautiful voices and are naturally talented musicians. A typical scene at a family reunion would be my uncle along with at least one of my cousins playing guitar, another on the piano, and about thirty of us gathered around and singing.

Both of my parents loved to read. Education was important, and studying was encouraged. Therefore, books were very important. The bottom shelves of our bookshelf were filled with Christian books, including the Bible. There was also a well-used set of encyclopedias, books about distant countries, and geography books. The top shelves were filled with some of the leading motivational and inspirational books by various authors. I remember on hot summer days looking forward to going to the local library and bringing home a stack of borrowed books, although I was not as studious as some of my older siblings. I chose some books for reading, but I chose many for the pictures, as I liked to draw and sketch a lot, especially animals and nature scenes. My dad's mother was a wonderful artist. As part of her legacy, she left her children many beautiful paintings of all sizes. Most of us have inherited her creativity and love for art.

Because my parents had a great interest in foreign countries and cultures, we often had foreign exchange students living with us and guests from overseas at our Thanksgiving or Christmas celebrations. Sometimes these guests from distant countries were invited by my older brothers and sisters while they were attending college. My mom was a fantastic cook, baker, and host and had the ability to make everyone feel welcome. "The more the merrier," it seemed. Later as our family grew, the holiday tables were also filled with in-laws, boyfriends, girlfriends, nieces, and nephews. I am still impressed that my mom could consistently host so many people and do this happily.

I believe the best gift my parents ever gave me was their strong faith. They both had a great love for God, Jesus, and the blessed Mother, Mary. I was raised in a traditional Roman Catholic family where we prayed together before every meal, went to church every Sunday, often prayed the rosary together, and attended Catholic grade school. My mother spoke often and openly about invoking saints and angels for particular prayer needs, and the walls of our home displayed pictures of Jesus, Mary, and the classic guardian angel prints. My dad had a strong devotion to the blessed Mother Mary and was particularly interested in Lourdes, Fatima, and Medjugorje, the most well-known places of Marian apparitions.

The lives of the saints were often discussed in our Catholic upbringing, and many of their lives involved great mysticism, healing, and miracles. As a Catholic, my understanding is that we do not worship saints and angels as we do God and Jesus. However, when we ask for their assistance, as they are in heaven and closer to God, our prayer requests are amplified and multiplied and therefore become more powerful.

My parents felt that their faith was often tested. On July 12, 1971, our entire farm, except for the house, was demolished when a tornado struck. It was called *The Saint Ansgar Tornado*. Fifteen farms were severely damaged, and more than five thousand acres of grain were destroyed. I can still remember that day very well. It was extremely hot and humid. In the late afternoon there was a downpour of rain that turned into baseball-sized hail. Then there was a brief period of eerie stillness and silence. My younger brother and I were playing cards in the living room where there were large picture windows on all sides. Suddenly we saw what looked like a massive wall of black dirt coming from the southwest toward us. All of the corn and small trees were pulled up by their roots and flew horizontal in unison straight across the air and into the wall of dirt. It sounded and felt like a powerful train was coming. My dad came into the house and told us all to get in the basement and take cover. This was not unusual, as there were a few tornado warnings and twisters hovering in the air every summer. However, this time the twister was on the ground and headed for our farm, and my brother Bob was missing, so my mom was panicking and screaming his name. As we waited for the tornado to pass, the outside cellar doors were slamming up and down. These two very heavy doors were especially built to withstand storms. There was an additional door down the steps on the inside. My mom started to run toward the door, hoping it was my brother, but my dad intercepted her and held her down. If she had opened it, she might have been pulled out into the eye of the storm.

My brother Bob, who was seventeen at the time, was working out in the field. When he saw the tornado coming toward the farm, he ran as fast as he could in the opposite direction. He said he thought he might have set some world record for running that day. Relieved, he watched as it missed our house. He held onto a fence post with all of his strength, his feet flailing in the air.

When the storm passed, we emerged from the basement to find complete devastation, except for the house. Most of our barns, silos, and sheds were destroyed, and many animals were lost. There were live electrical wires strewn around and several annoying news reporters.

Naturally my mom was completely distraught for some time. However, my parents immediately saw the tremendous blessing that all of us were still alive and no one was injured. They were also extremely grateful that our house was still standing. There were only a few cracks in the walls and some broken windows.

We witnessed an incredible outpouring of love from our neighbors and relatives. Many people from the community and neighborhood came to show their support. The men helped to remove the debris, and the women brought their very best offering of homemade food. Throughout those hot summer days they also brought gallons of lemonade to help cool the farmers who were helping. This tradition of supporting each other in this small farming community is one reason why I treasure it!

I have been aware from a fairly young age that I see people differently than some others do. I believe I look at people from a soul level, and I often have an understanding of what is in their hearts. Already when I was in the fourth grade, people seemed to recognize this and would often tell me their deepest secrets almost everywhere I went. They would usually say they didn't even know why they felt compelled to confess these things to me, as they had not ever told anyone else. Most of the time I didn't mind. It became slightly more puzzling as I became older, and now those telling me their secrets were my husband's boss, the administrator for the hospital where I was working, or other authority figures.

It is only in recent years that I understand that I was a *sensitive* child from the earliest time I can remember. I do not mean that I was overly emotional, but I was sensitive to positive and negative energy. I often had dreams of aunts and uncles shortly before or after they passed away. I remember *feeling* spirits at nighttime and often praying to St. Michael for protection from the time I was in the second grade and could read. It was at the beginning of the third grade that I remember occasionally hearing messages about God, especially in church or religion class, if I got lost in thought. They still stand out very clearly in my mind, and I remember that they were loud, clear, and consistent messages that left a strong impression.

While I was in college, the church and youth center at Saint Thomas Aquinas at Iowa State University became my second home. The priests there often encouraged me to become a nun. I heard a loving voice in my head saying, "No, in this life you want to have a family. You have already done that often enough." I wondered, *What? This life?* I sang as a worship leader there usually twice a week. Before rehearsal I would often sit in the church for hours and just talk to God. I felt tremendous peace there. I wondered why the church wasn't filled with people at all times. That was the first time I questioned, "Doesn't everyone feel what I feel?" I believed until only a few years ago that everyone could feel what I felt, hear what I heard, and see what I saw.

All of this being said, there were plenty of times that I did all of the normal things that teenagers did while they were growing up. I definitely had my rebellious phases. Sometimes it was because I was tired of people saying that I looked and acted so innocent and I just wanted to be like everyone else.

One thing that influenced my youth was that I was slightly overweight and teased a lot as a child. My mom took me to the doctor when I was around eight years old. I remember her saying, "I don't understand. She eats and plays the same as the other children, but she just keeps gaining weight. No one else in the family is overweight." I was referred to a dietitian who put me on my first thousand-calorie diet. My weight went up and down, and so did the teasing and bullying accordingly.

Fortunately making friends has always been fairly easy for me regardless of my weight. I am thankful to have always had a great group of good friends. We were together from the first through the twelfth grade. I believe I am naturally open and friendly, and I like to laugh a lot. I consider myself to be levelheaded, and people have often told me that I am a good listener and have a calming effect on them. I do not like drama or conflict. I enjoy peace and freedom.

My weight skyrocketed around the age of thirteen. I was desperate for the pain of being teased to stop. I started reading a lot about nutrition, and it really interested me. I prayed to God for help, and I said several novenas to St. Jude Thaddeus, the saint of miracles for lost causes and hopeless cases. A novena is a set of specific prayers that one says over a number of days. I had often witnessed my mom praying in this way as I was growing up, and she spoke very openly about it. With such a large family there were always prayer needs. She lit a votive candle to aid in a prayer request almost daily. Next to the candle were always pictures displayed of whom she was praying to. That being said, there was one time that she was so angry when we had three consecutive storms that blew down her three favorite beautiful large shade trees, and I saw her throw that candle out the door. She threw it as far as she could onto the lawn. However, later in the day she retrieved it. And the very next day she lit it again. Whatever storms appeared in their lives—and there were many—my parents always maintained their faith.

By the time I turned fifteen, I had acquired the knowledge, motivation, and strength to lose about a hundred pounds before my sixteenth birthday. I noticed how much food affected my energy level. I stopped eating all processed food and anything with white sugar and flour. I ate only vegetables, fruit, and lean protein, and I started walking a little every day. This led to power-walking one hour a day. I set new goals for myself every week and was eventually jogging two to five miles most every day.

I was on the volleyball team in high school all four years. I remember how difficult it was for me to run laps my freshman and sophomore year. I was usually one of the last in line. Then when I returned for practice my junior year, I had jogged so much that summer that I felt like I could run forever! My coach was really proud of me. I remember what a sense of accomplishment and freedom I felt.

My life changed in many ways. I was much healthier, and the teasing stopped. Instead there were many nice boys knocking on our door. Most importantly I felt losing the weight increased my confidence enough that I was free to be who I was meant to be. By my senior year I was president of my high school class, the choir, honor society, and student council. I was also very active in the marching and concert bands, show choir, journalism, and drama club. There were only 110 people in my graduating class, so it was easy to be involved.

I decided that I wanted to become a dietitian. I saw how altering my diet completely changed my health and my life, and I wanted to help others to do the same. It seemed very unfair to me that so many people felt as though they had the right to tell me that I was overweight and were mean to me because of it. Now many of these same people treated me like I was a different person after I became thin. I was the same person. I wanted to be someone who would be there for the overweight people who felt they had no one to encourage them.

Although singing was my passion and I had a few scholarship opportunities to study music, I had seen several extremely talented girls from my hometown have difficulties finding a job after they had majored in music. Therefore, I felt that I needed to do something practical. Having several older siblings in a medical profession, I followed in their footsteps. When I took the career aptitude and personality tests to see which career would be a good choice for me according to my strengths and interests, *registered dietitian* appeared in the number-one position.

The Streit kids on the farm in 1967

My First Angelic Experience—Proof of a Spiritual World

Even though I believed in angels, I was not completely sure if they existed in our day and age, so I was completely surprised and somewhat startled when I had my first angelic experience in 1986, an encounter that possibly saved my life.

I was excited to be accepted into an accelerated dietetics program that combined a great deal of practical work experience with the necessary academic courses. I needed a summer work experience for my major at Iowa State University, which was food and nutrition/dietetics with a minor in hotel and restaurant management. As there were few job opportunities in rural Iowa, I took a summer job working at a big camp near Ames, Iowa.

I was hired by a large organization to prepare meals for four hundred girls and thirty-five staff every day. I was enthusiastically told in the interview that I and the other two cooks would have our own house to live in on the campsite.

Upon my arrival I was disappointed to find my summer home would be an old trailer house. The other two more experienced women arrived before me and rightly claimed the bigger bedrooms near the front of the trailer. The remaining bedroom was a small room at the very back. The room was empty except for a simple cot and a closet. After I checked out my new work environment, including the building that housed a very large cafeteria and a nice industrial-sized kitchen, I unpacked my belongings. I then displayed, with the help of some mounting putty, about forty of my favorite photographs of family and friends.

Before I turned out the light to sleep, I heard a voice that said, "Take down your photographs and put them, your wallet, and your car keys into your brown leather bag." I ignored it and turned off the light with the intention of going to sleep. Suddenly my bed started shaking and then rocking back and forth. I heard the voice again, and this time it was louder. As strange as it sounds, I was not afraid but rather calm. This voice was familiar to me, as I had heard it when I was younger. As it was pitch black, I reached for my flashlight and looked to see if there was a big raccoon or other animal under my bed. I had lived a previous summer in a tent for three months while I was working as a camp counselor and sometimes there were raccoons that came into our tent at night. Then my bed rocked swiftly back and forth and literally rocked me out of the bed and onto my feet. I heard the same voice again, but this time it was louder and more authoritative. It said, "Take down your photographs and put them, your wallet, and your car keys into your leather bag!" Finally I obeyed the voice, and I did as it said. Again what was especially odd was that this voice did not frighten but rather calmed me. I also did not think at the time that this was particularly strange. Surprisingly I fell asleep right away and slept well through the rest of the night.

The next morning I felt as though someone gently nudged me awake. I felt a calm urgency to get out the door and to work. The ladies and I left the trailer house around 7:10 a.m. to prepare our first meal together for the staff. We had just walked about fifteen or twenty feet from the trailer when we heard a loud explosion. We turned around to see the entire building engulfed in flames. Everything in the trailer was completely gone in about ten minutes, with only the frame remaining. Except for the items I put into the brown leather bag, I lost everything I owned, which was not nearly as much as the other two semiretired women.

What had been my room for one night was now mostly ashes. On top of the ashes was my leather bag with all of the things that were most important to me—the car keys, my photographs, and my wallet. The bag was completely untouched. Remarkably, it appeared as though someone had placed it on top of the ashes.

When the firemen came, they told us repeatedly how lucky we were to be alive. It was as if they could not emphasize it enough. They said that if we had left the trailer just one or two minutes later, we probably would not have made it out on time. They told me that I was especially fortunate, as the back door of the trailer, which was in my room, had been nailed shut and it would have been impossible for me to escape. They repeatedly emphasized to me how lucky I was to be alive. After investigating, they discovered that the entire wiring of the trailer home was aluminum and therefore was not legal. That was the reason that the fire started and spread so rapidly.

I had seen something similar to this when I was quite young, and it left an impression on me. Our farmhouse caught on fire while my little brother John was alone in the house and napping upstairs. Fortunately my eldest brother, Dave, was home on leave from the US Air Force. He was outside working and saw the smoke and called the fire department. My mom, my sisters, and I were at the neighbors about two miles away, when we heard and saw the fire trucks rushing by. My mom instinctively knew that they were headed to our house, and her focus immediately turned to my little brother. We thought that she was negatively overreacting. She immediately started praying out loud and called on his guardian angels to protect him. Thankfully he was fine. After the firemen left, we saw how the entire walls of the large room where the fire had been were ruined and black, but the crucifix and other religious artifacts hanging on the walls were untouched. The wall directly behind the crucifix was also unscathed. She pointed this out to me and told me how she had heard of similar stories from others who had fires in their homes. She felt that my oldest brother had saved my youngest brother's life that day, possibly with help from his guardian angel.

After the firemen left the camp-site that day, I knew without a doubt that it had been an angel that had helped me that night by sparing my most valuable items, and that angel had possibly saved my life that morning. It gave me proof of an invisible spiritual world. This was comforting but at the same time slightly unsettling. I knew that it was a real experience. However, as I was not comfortable talking about it, about the only one I shared this with was my best friend and roommate in college. Her faith was strong, and she wasn't afraid to talk about it with me.

Following the fire, I felt that there was a reason that my life was spared and that there was something important that I was supposed to do, but I had no idea what it was. It also caused me to think about the bigger questions in life like *What is the purpose of my life? Why am I here?* That was the first time I remember asking God, "What do you want me to do?"

That afternoon we were given a company sweat suit to wear and taken in a van to the company headquarters in Des Moines. We were brought to the office of a tough woman named Jo. I think she could have had a good career in the military. She scolded us and told us that the fire never happened. She threatened us and told us that we were not to tell anyone about this and to completely forget about it.

I was shocked. It was wrong. I believe that Jo was reacting to fear and the possibility that her job and company might be compromised. If word got out that a building had exploded and gone up in flames on this company's campground, then some of the parents who were supposed to send their girls to this camp for the summer may change their minds, and the organization could potentially lose a lot of money.

Upon our return I was temporarily moved into a cabin that looked as though it had not been occupied for several years. The front door was boarded up. There were, to my unfortunate surprise, many large rats inhabiting this cabin. And now it seemed I was invading their home. Having grown up on a farm with seven older brothers and sisters, I am not a wimpy girl. I am quite flexible and can tolerate a lot. However, having large rats run over me that night was too much for me. After they chewed a hole through a thick plastic container to my one and only new possession, a pair of underwear, I set traps. The only man working at the camp arranged the traps for me. Unfortunately they were only big enough to slightly slow them down and anger them. I pushed the trapped rats out the door with a baseball bat while they were hissing loudly at me.

When I look back now, I think, *Why in the world did I stay there, and why did I not go back to my parents home for the summer?* One reason was that I had signed a contract to do a job and I didn't want to quit. Another was that I needed the summer work experience for my internship, and I needed the money I was going to earn for college. The other major reason was that I did not want to tell my parents about the fire and burden them. This was because we were all grieving as my eldest sister, Mary, had been diagnosed a few months before that with terminal cancer. Mary was an extremely kind, generous, funny, and loving sister. Because she was twelve years older than me, she was like a wonderful and cool second mom to us younger kids. She had the gift of knowing exactly what to do or say to help me or make me feel accepted and safe. We didn't receive many presents when I was young or new clothing, but I remember every present she ever gave me, as it was always exactly what I really needed or wanted, such as a set of sketching supplies or a beautiful nightgown. She *saw* me and was always very thoughtful. Now she had a very fast-spreading cancer, and she had just been placed on an artificial ventilator just a few days before I left to work at the camp. So I did not want to worry my parents unnecessarily, as I was not in any danger now.

As the supplies at the camp were very sparse, with only one telephone accessible at the front office and only the bare necessities available, I was very grateful that three of my brothers lived an hour away at the time and came to visit me. Each of them brought something to help me out or to cheer me up. My older brother Bob brought me some secondhand clothes. My brother Wayne, whose small pickup truck I was borrowing, filled it with gas and brought me a stuffed animal. And my youngest and closest brother, John, brought me a box of practical items like pens, paper, and pencils. Not having anything but the company sweat suit and the clothes I was wearing at the time of the fire, I was very thankful for everything. I had never been so happy to receive a pencil before in my life. The fire definitely made me appreciate everything even more. It took several years until I did not fear fire or briefly envision my apartment building engulfed in flames when I returned home from work.

Karen after the fire

My First Open Vision—The Praying Hands

A few days after the fire and the episode with the rats, we were moved into a replacement trailer. As I did not want to sleep in the rear bedroom, I slept on a sleeping bag in the front kitchen area. That very first night I woke up in the middle of the night with the most incredible hunger I had ever experienced, and it would not go away. I felt like I was starving and had not eaten for days. It was not like normal hunger. I wondered if the shock of the fire and then being wrongfully scolded had allowed something foreign to enter my body. It felt as though there was now a huge monster living inside of me, and it was starving! I found myself having to eat every couple of hours to avoid this unusual hunger. If I did not eat, I became very confused and faint. It was very frightening to suddenly feel confused as if no glucose was getting to my brain. This made me angry, as I had worked so hard to get off and keep off any extra weight, and this meant I needed to increase my daily one or two-hour workouts to avoid gaining weight.

13

The symptoms continued for many months. After I collapsed on campus twice, I went to the university clinic. The doctor administered a five-hour glucose tolerance test. It was very difficult for me because I needed to drink a sugary beverage, and my body responded very poorly. I realized that I was very sensitive to sugar when I was around fourteen years old and had completely avoided it since that time. The test revealed severe hypoglycemia (low blood sugar). As the physician had never seen such an abnormal test, he suggested I repeat the test the following week. After a second highly abnormal test he advised me to go to the Mayo Clinic in Rochester, Minnesota, for further evaluation, and he made all of the necessary arrangements for me.

I had three days of medical tests the next summer after I graduated and before I began working. Normal blood glucose levels range between 80–120 mg/dl and slightly higher during the two hours after a meal. Because my blood sugar levels were plummeting every few hours down to 30 mg/dl, the endocrinologist thought I must have an insulin-secreting pancreatic tumor. He wanted to be certain that I would not go into a coma. The doctor administered drugs, one being tolbutamide, more commonly known as Orinase, which is an oral hypoglycemic agent and causes the pancreas to quickly produce insulin and therefore lower the blood sugar. He wanted to observe how my body responded and if it could recover on its own. Because insulin is a hormone, this felt like torture, and it was agonizing emotionally. He believed that if I had a tumor, it was most likely cancerous. And even if it were benign, he recommended removing the tumor and my pancreas. This meant that I would be diabetic for the rest of my life. I do not know if these would be the normal evaluation tests that would still be used today or if I received these because I had a doctor from overseas whose reasoning was different than the norm. Once again I did not tell my parents or brothers and sisters about the severity of my possible diagnosis, as my sister Mary had passed away the previous October from colon cancer and we were all still grieving. As she had worked for many years at the Mayo Clinic as a medical technologist, I imagine it must have been difficult for my mom to accompany me to those medical tests.

The night before I was supposed to receive the prognosis, I could not sleep because I was so worried. I remained awake and prayed every prayer I knew. I had a stack of prayer books and had been on my knees for hours in my bedroom. Of course I didn't want to have cancer or be diabetic, but I also knew how my entire family was still heartbroken after the loss of my sister, so I prayed to be healed.

I had my first open vision while I was lying in bed around 3:30 a.m. It was of the image of the praying hands over the area of my stomach and abdomen. They were much larger than normal human hands and were emanating soft white light. I heard, "All is well. Everything will be all right." With this vision and these words, I knew that I was going to be fine. My worry vanished in an instant, and I fell asleep.

The next day I received the diagnosis of severe hypoglycemia of unknown etiology. Thankfully there was no evidence of a tumor, and he had no idea why this was occurring. The doctor said he had never seen anything like this before. I was instructed on following a diabetic diet and was told to eat five small meals a day to keep my blood sugar stable. I was given a glucagon kit for emergencies and a glucometer to measure my blood sugar regularly. Diabetes had been of particular interest to me as a student, and I had studied the diet extensively and instructed many patients on it as part of my internship in a large hospital. I did not know at that time how valuable this information would be to me personally.

I wish I could say that after the vision of the large praying hands over my body, the severe hunger and the symptoms from the low blood glucose levels disappeared, but they didn't. However, I was extremely thankful that I did not need an operation and that I was not diabetic.

I was evaluated once more in 1991 and participated in a three-day starvation test while I was monitored in the hospital. They monitored my blood glucose levels for one day while I was eating normally and then throughout three days while I was eating nothing and drinking only water. Unfortunately there was no success in determining why my blood sugar consistently dropped dangerously low. They told me that my blood sugar dropped two hours after every meal to a level that it would normally fall to after not eating anything for three days. It has, however, continuously improved in recent years with the more healing I have received.

I do not know what I have been spared from in my life, but I believe that most of us have been spared from many things that we aren't even aware of. And our prayers have been answered but not in ways that are always evident to us immediately. Today after many years of experience with life and death and angels, I believe that angels are not just *nice* occasional helpers but that their presence is actually vital for our survival upon the earth, and that is why every person comes into the world with at least two.

Move to Minneapolis

A few weeks later in September of 1987, I moved to Minneapolis, Minnesota, and secured a job working as a registered dietitian in a northern suburb. Although it was only my first interview, I liked the administrator who was conducting the interview, and I had a good feeling, so I accepted the offer. I was hired as the director of dietary at Camilia Rose, a long-term care and rehabilitation center. I was the youngest of seventeen departmental directors and was responsible for determining the nutritional care of 120 clients, managing the dietary department, including forty-five employees, as well as educating the entire staff on nutrition.

I liked my job a lot. I felt very honored to have been awarded employee of the month after a few months and employee of the year a year after that. This was voted on by all of the employees and clients. I felt well accepted and was very grateful.

The main reason I mention these positive highlights of my life is not to boast. It is because I have continuously felt that throughout my lifetime whenever I got knocked down, God always picked me up and made up for it in unexpected ways. Throughout any hardship, I always received blessings to boost my spirit and enable me to believe that regardless of what happened, I would land on my feet.

My direct boss at Camilia Rose was the administrator, Norma. She had very high expectations of all of the directors. I am still grateful to her, as she was a fantastic mentor. I respected her as she lived by her own standards and set a great example. She commanded excellent quality and service. Under her direction I underwent many hours of management training and taught weekly classes on nutrition. I especially enjoyed teaching. Norma recognized this and encouraged me to teach on a broader basis. Because of this, I also taught several classes at a local community college, as well as at some bigger healthcare conferences.

Norma began her career as a nurse. Because her father was an alcoholic, she had a great interest in alternative healing as well as conventional Western medicine. She believed that most health-care workers have very nurturing and sometimes codependent personalities and often come from dysfunctional families. Therefore, she invited many excellent motivational and self-empowerment speakers into the company. They offered presentations and workshops relating to alternative health and healing. Everyone was encouraged to attend for free. Some of them spoke about using the newest approaches that involved positive affirmations, visualization, and meditation as tools for self-empowerment.

It was then that I first began to incorporate meditation, positive affirmations, and self-hypnosis into the weight-loss classes that were offered to the staff. With the addition of these new tools along with the daily lunch-hour power walks, many of my coworkers had great weight-loss results. I felt that these new tools also helped me in many ways, and I was very happy in every way.

The Love of My Life

I met Michael on December 8, 1989, through mutual good friends. My two roommates and I had a Christmas party, and he was invited. When he rang the doorbell, I opened the door, and it was love at first sight. I took one look into his brown eyes and seriously felt like I had known him for a thousand years. I had never felt this way before. Nor would I have believed that this was even possible. I was on cloud nine. I did not find him to be particularly good-looking; however, it was his words that enchanted me, and I was attracted to him like a magnet. I met him ten days before he was supposed to move back to his home country of Germany. He had lived in Minneapolis for the previous year and a half, establishing the first American subsidiary for a company in Germany.

I found him to be extremely charming, kind, funny, and intelligent. I thought, *Wow, someone who can converse with my family!* He completely swept me off my feet. We went on a few dates in the ten days before he left. After he moved back to his hometown, he showered me with daily love letters, red roses, and weekly phone calls. He seemed to be the perfect mixture of a good-natured farm boy and a sharp businessman. I found his quirky cultural differences to be intriguing and charming. The attraction was so strong that I felt I had almost no choice in the matter. I followed my heart, and my heart wanted to stay by his side forever.

I brought him home and introduced him to my family the following July. I had never seen my mom so smitten with anyone. She said he reminded her of a young Omar Sharif. My little brother said we were both "googly-eyed" as we admired him while he was talking. Her approval was very important to me. My mom said to me after she met him, "Karen, I would follow him to the end of the world!" That is exactly what I ended up doing—following him to the other side of the world.

I was genuinely so in love I felt like I wanted to be with him even if he lived somewhere in a cave. When I arrived for the first time to visit him in Germany in May of 1990, I discovered that he did not live in a cave at all. By mentioning the following, I am not meaning to sound arrogant, as cars and brands have never meant much to me, but I would like to give you an idea of how extremely fun and exciting this time with him was.

He picked me up at the Frankfurt airport in a burgundy Porsche Carrera. He drove me straight to a very large and impressive abbey near his hometown called Kloster Schöntal (abbey of the beautiful valley). This abbey is one of the most famous pieces of Baroque architecture in his state and was founded in 1153. It is exquisitely beautiful and very ornate. He took me near the striking altar gate and said, "This is where my grandparents and my parents were both married, and this is where I want to marry you!" I was stunned. The logical part of me wanted to say, "Now wait a minute!" And the other part wanted to happily scream, "Yes, I do!"

We then drove to his parents' home. We walked up about thirty stone steps through a beautiful flower garden before we reached the front door. There were many lovely flowering bushes and trees that I had never seen before. Their large home had a distinct rustic elegance and a lovely view onto the Kocher River, vineyards, and the valley below. I instantly liked them very much. After this I met more of his relatives and friends. I was warmly greeted everywhere we went.

We drove on what is known as the "Romantic Road" through the spectacular countryside and on to Munich. After we visited several lovely castles in Bavaria, he took me to meet his sister, who was living in Paris at the time. Every day was a new adventure and a new celebration. There was a party for us everywhere we went, and he was the life of it. He lived life *large* and seemed to have no fear. I admired his strong self-confidence because he appeared to remain so humble. I had never met anyone like this before. I felt like the luckiest girl in the world to have met my soul mate and the love of my life. I was not happy that he was from another country, but I still considered myself to be fortunate. I thought, *What are the chances of me meeting my soul-mate from Germany and us both falling instantly in love?*

After this magical whirlwind romance we were married on May 11, 1991, in my hometown in Iowa. Very soon after we met, he told me he loved me and asked me to move to Germany, but I preferred to do things right. I wanted a proper wedding in my hometown church. His immediate family, grandma, and best friend came to Iowa for the wedding.

After our American wedding my entire family flew to Germany for a family vacation and a second wedding in Germany. It was shortly after the first Gulf War had ended, and flight prices were very reasonable. We assembled a tour of all the nicest sites in Southern Germany, Austria, and Switzerland and called it the Van-Streit Family Tour, as Streit is my maiden name. I think we all had a fantastic time, and it was wonderful to explore that part of Europe for ten days together. Although some of us had visited Europe before, having had very little material means while growing up, I had not thought when I was younger that this would someday be possible.

Two weeks after our American wedding we had another wedding for his relatives in the beautiful abbey, Kloster Schöntal, near his hometown. The setting was so spectacular that I felt like I was in a fairy tale. It was the same ceremony in German but without the actual sacrament of marriage. His dad's men's choir sang beautifully from a balcony high above. We all thoroughly enjoyed the traditional German wedding festivities, which were lively and quite different than the ones in America. There was a bountiful celebration with plenty of fine local wine and delicious customary cuisine offered, many songs sung, poems recited, and skits performed, as well as around twenty fancy homemade cakes served. Festivals are a big part of the German culture, and ours lasted until dawn, which I later learned was typical.

Michael and I at Kloster Schöntal, Germany

Move to Germany

Throughout our courtship Michael continually tried to convince me to move to Germany. I was quite hesitant, as I was very happy where I was living. I loved being relatively close to my family, I really enjoyed the Minnesota lakes, and I liked my job a lot. I finally agreed to move to Germany for one year after we were married. My mom and I both cried together when I told her the news. She was afraid that I would not come back after one year as I had thought. She was right.

This new life with Michael began twenty-two years that would bring one major global adventure after another. I feel as though I have had enough experiences for ten lives during these last twenty-two years. I somehow knew that being married to him would never be boring, but I had not expected that my life would become an extreme of the best and worst that life could possibly offer. After a few years of marriage I felt as though I had accidentally stepped onto a high-speed mega roller coaster and I was longing for safety and stability. He told me when I met him that he worked and traveled a lot, but I did not know that this meant he would be gone for two weeks at a time most of the time.

My family departed back to the United States the Monday after our German wedding, and Michael left the next day for an extended business trip. As the apartment we were supposed to move into in nearby Schwäbisch Hall was delayed in being renovated, we lived with his parents for the first two months. Because I was mostly alone with his mom, who did not speak any English, I learned more German in that first week after the German wedding than I did in the twelve weeks of German language classes prior to moving to Germany.

His mom had to laugh many times at my bumbling attempts to speak German. I learned many things during those first months, including how to cook a wide variety of traditional dishes, dozens of unwritten rules that are a very important part of their culture, and the fact that perfection and punctuality were critical and expected at all times. There seemed to be an unwritten rule for everything, and there was no room for variation. Only what was traditional was acceptable. There were rules and specific days of the week for when to shower or bath, shampoo your hair, sweep the street outside your home, clean the outdoor and indoor staircases, wash the windows, and launder each particular type of clothing, just to name of few. Although I appreciated the strict organization and cleanliness and realized the necessity of it in such a densely populated country, I found it to be confining, as I was taught from a young age to be independent and make my best decision based on my own reasoning. Because I was considered wrong if I was different in any way or did not comply with all of these rules, I felt as though my personal power was slowly stripped away from me. I wondered if this was what military boot camp felt like, in regards to the mental re-conditioning. Because I was taught to respect my elders and not to voice my opinion or make waves, I thought it was the right thing to accept this controlling behavior and and I did not complain. I did my very best to comply and fit in.

Before I could find a job, I needed to improve my German, so I attended the Goethe Institute in Schwäbisch Hall for two months. I participated in intense, full-time language courses. There were around thirty adult students from all over the world in my class, and I liked it a lot. It was a little like being back in college, except we were ages twenty-two to sixty. All of us became quite close, but when the summer was over, they all went home to their respective countries.

Throughout these early years of our marriage when Michael was not traveling, part of his job as a salesman was entertaining guests from all over the world. He was a fantastic showman! This was often very interesting for me when I was invited to join them on excursions. Occasionally he had unexpected visitors, and he needed my assistance to entertain them. There was one time when the guests were three men from the Middle East. I took them to see the nicest sites in our area. We went to Rothenburg, one of the most well-preserved medieval cities in Europe with the original city wall still intact. I then showed them the Residenz in Würzburg, a lovely palace that was owned by the prince-bishop of Würzburg. I also took them to the Abbey Schöntal, where we were married. Throughout the entire day they did not say one word. I was not sure if they spoke English or if they didn't care for any of the places that we visited. They appeared to be pale and almost numb with fear. Then it dawned on me. I was not thinking about how strange and uncomfortable this may have possibly been for them to have a talkative white woman pick them up and drive them around, dressed in normal clothing. The cultural differences must have been shocking. I'm sure in their eyes I had possibly broken many traditions. I said a quick prayer and felt that I heard an answer. I found a restaurant that I thought might serve close to what would be their traditional food. When we sat down, I asked them if they would tell me about their faith. Then it was as if I had turned on a gushing water faucet that had previously been stuck. They could hardly speak enough. They spoke English perfectly. They shared their beliefs with me for a few hours, and we had a lovely evening. This left an impression on me, as their beliefs and love for God were much more similar to mine than I would have ever realized.

Following that first summer I was happy to get a job at a very large local hospital. I should have possibly known something was awry when they so quickly hired me to be the dietary director and put me in charge of the large kitchen and the nutritional care of the patients. I discovered on my first day that they had recently had a huge salmonella outbreak with more than half of the kitchen staff being hospitalized. It was complete chaos and very stressful in the kitchen, and the personnel were all shouting at one another. As no one spoke English and most of the staff spoke German with a very strong Schwäbisch dialect, it was initially very difficult for me to understand them. I was only cooking, as there was no time for counseling the patients on nutrition. In addition, my required uniform was a rather short white dress, which felt rather degrading. Since the time of my college internship, I was used to wearing a nice dress with a white lab coat over it.

I had worked straight through the weekends for about nine weeks in a row and was working late one evening. Three bulky men of Russian descent from the night staff came into the kitchen and started taunting me with explicit phrases. They formed a circle around me and assaulted me. I am only five-foot-two, and I weighed 110 pounds at the time; however, my adrenaline kicked in, and I put my knees and elbows to good use and broke free. I left immediately and quit the job the next morning. They initially refused to let me break my contract until I told them what had happened. I think it was the first time I had ever quit anything in my life.

It seemed the honeymoon was over. It was much more difficult than I thought it would be to be away from my family and friends and submerged in a different culture. I felt complete loss for everyone and everything I missed in America, and I did not realize how different the culture could be. Where I am from in Iowa, most people are very proud of their German heritage. The annual festival in my hometown of Stacyville is even called "Bratwurst and Sauerkraut Daze." I didn't realize the mentality could be so different. Although Michael had told me before we were married that he worked and traveled a lot, it was not clear to me that this meant that I would be alone most of the time. I also did not know how consistently stressed out he would be because of his job when he was home.

I believe Michael did not know how to help or support me when it was evident that I was experiencing loss for my former life in America, and so he tried the art of distraction and asked me to accompany him the following weekend to a trade show in Cairo, Egypt. This trip was very interesting and exciting. I appreciated seeing him in action, and it helped me to better understand the demands of his job more fully. This was my earliest, most impressionable experience of meeting people from various places in Africa and the Middle East, seeing extreme poverty first-hand, and recognizing some enormous differences and other surprising commonalities that we shared. At one point, we were seated on large comfortable cushions in a tent at this large trade show. Michael was involved in a lively political discussion with the men while I silently observed from the back of the tent, alone. I feel this symbolized well the place I would take throughout the course of our marriage.

We enjoyed seeing the pyramids of Giza and the Great Sphinx and were photographed on camels in front of them. I was able to visit several sacred sites, including an ancient church dating back to the time of Christ called St. Sergius. It is believed that this was where Jesus, Mary, and Joseph lived after they fled from King Herod. I was surprised to see some original ancient Coptic iconic paintings of several of the same images that my mom always kept in the kitchen near her votive candle. This became my tradition whenever I was accompanying Michael to a new city or country throughout our marriage. I would seek out the sacred sites and visit them independently while he was busy with meetings.

Me in Cairo, Egypt

Very soon after returning from this trip, I received some wonderful gifts. I have been singing in church since I was around twelve years old. Michael's younger brother was the organist at their church in their hometown and he invited me to sing many Sundays from the time of my arrival in Germany. I appreciated this very much, and this also helped to improve my German. At this time Michael had the idea of placing an advertisement in the newspaper for myself as a wedding singer. And it worked! I started receiving one phone call after another to sing at weddings. Word quickly spread, and I was traveling to little villages and bigger cities to sing almost every Saturday afternoon. It was usually very interesting, and I met great people and many wonderful musicians. Every wedding was a new adventure. Sometimes it was in a small country church and other times in a large cathedral or a historical old chapel that was part of a large castle.

I began singing at weddings as a teenager. I was in college when people who heard me sing at church began offering me transportation, flight tickets, and payment to sing at their weddings. I traveled to several states that I had never visited before. Later, I was on the liturgy commission at my church in Minneapolis and my church in college, and I had several years of experience helping couples plan their wedding music. It was natural for me and it flowed easily. Throughout the last twenty-two years I had the opportunity to sing in many large cathedrals, castles, a beautiful chapel in the Alps near Zurich, Switzerland, and even as a soloist at Kloster Schöntal, where we were married. Sometimes I had to pinch myself, as I could not believe the marvelous and historical places I had the opportunity to sing at. It was very rewarding. I continued to do this and was booked most spring, summer, and fall Saturdays whenever we lived in Germany until I departed in 2012.

One of the greatest gifts I was given was meeting members of a choir who became my wonderful and lifelong friends. I had been asked to sing two songs at a wedding as a surprise to the bride, and a youth choir was also asked to sing two songs. I had been searching for a church choir for months, but this was the first choir I heard that I really liked. The choir's name was Crescendo. They had a unique gospel sound, and their quality was excellent. A few of the members came up to me after the wedding service and asked me to join their choir. Although my first impression was very good, I was hesitant, as I still could not understand all of the heavy dialects spoken in that area. I wondered if I could understand the choir director's instructions. My speaking voice sounds like that of a child, but my singing voice can be powerful, so the possibility of a loud mistake in public is elevated. After several more invitations by phone I attended their choir rehearsal, and I am very thankful that I did. I cherish every moment that I was able to spend with them. They were consistently accepting and loving toward me all of these years.

The next major gift I received was meeting my best American friend in Germany. I met her shortly after this. One night I could not help crying as Michael had been traveling a lot and was very stressed from his work when he was home. As he had no time to offer me support, I told him that I really needed a good girlfriend and I prayed for one. The very next day there was a note in my mailbox from a woman named Mary from Long Island, New York. She was the president of the American-European Dietetic Association and had seen my name on a list of American dietitians living in Europe. I called her right away, and we talked for more than two hours. She lived only ten minutes away from where we were living, and she was also married to a German man who had a position and disposition similar to Michael's, so we had a lot in common. She became my dearest friend. She had recently met another American woman named Lori from Oregon, so now there were three of us. We went for walks together and celebrated birthdays and American holidays as a family. They were like sisters to me for as long as I resided in Germany. Later our children were all born around the same time, and they became close as well.

Mary helped me in many ways over the years. When I met her in the fall of 1991, she had a great job at the US Air Force base in Schwaebisch Hall as a customer service agent at the bank on the base. She encouraged me to apply. I was hired at the bank at the US Army base in Crailsheim, which was about thirty minutes away. I liked this job much more than the hospital, and the salary was double.

While I was working there, I was honored to receive the Commander's Award for Outstanding Customer Service. There was a very nice ceremony, and I received official military medals. My boss and the director of the bank, who were both German, appeared to be fairly angry. They had worked there for many years and had never received an award. I thought I could almost see the steam coming out of their ears. There was a big draw down on American military troops in Europe the next year, and both bases closed in September of 1993.

Another huge way that Mary helped me was to involve me with the American-European Dietetic Association. I volunteered to plan conferences held in cities throughout Europe. I was later voted onto the board of directors. The annual board meetings were held in London, which was an incredible opportunity, as I love London. Mary and I had the chance to explore the city together. We especially appreciated the politeness and predominantly delightful demeanor of the British people. This was a respite from the abrupt disposition of some of those living in Germany. In addition, it was like a breath of fresh air to hear and speak English again. However, Michael preferred me to be home and did not want me to be gone or traveling, and so he encouraged me to give up dietetics, as he thought I would never need it again. He wanted to provide enough for both of us. I did not agree at that time. But later after we moved to Asia, it became very difficult for me to obtain the educational requirements to maintain my registration and licensure. There were no online classes available at that time.

After the military bases closed in the fall of 1993, I secured a job assisting a mechanical engineer for a newly established company handling ventilation products of many varieties. My first boss was a very good family man, and I liked him a lot. He spoke little English and had a very heavy dialect, so my German really improved at this point. I learned words like *Ventilstosselplaetzen*. I did well and liked this job.

Then one day about a year later, the president of the company called me into his office and told me that I would now be working for him. His secretary's desk was moved to the far end of his large office, and mine was placed directly next to his. She was red with fury. He proceeded to tell me, "Frau Bauer, now that you work for me, you have to sleep with me."

I said, "*Wie, bitte?*" meaning, "Excuse me?" He repeated it. I was shocked and practically speechless. I said the only thing that came to mind, which was, "*Nicht is diesem Leben*," which meant, "Not in this lifetime!" I left immediately and went to see my mother-in-law. Michael was traveling, and I was upset.

I told her about it, and she said, "Well, did you?"

I said, "Of course not!" She did not seem overly surprised or appalled. This reaction was very puzzling to me. I thought about how differently my own mom would have responded. It made me wonder if something was wrong with me because I found it so upsetting. It was right after this that Michael was asked by his boss to move to Singapore.

His Dream Come True

When Michael proposed to me in 1990, he told me his dreams of one day living in Singapore, Australia, and South Africa. He had been to all of these places and was fascinated by them. I did not take it very seriously, as I did not yet know how determined he was. Nor did I know how skillful he was at manifesting his dreams.

We moved from Germany to Singapore in September of 1995. Michael was asked by his boss to investigate the Singaporean subsidiary because there was suspicion of money laundering and embezzlement. Because of the two negative incidences that I had recently experienced at work and the sometimes-stifling atmosphere of the rigid culture, I was excited for a change and was genuinely happy to support him in the pursuit of his dreams. We were supposed to move there for one year.

The Republic of Singapore is in Southeast Asia and is located just off the southern tip of the peninsula of Malaysia. On a globe or a map of the world it is represented by a very small dot that is almost exactly on the opposite side of the world from Iowa. It consists of the main island of Singapore and around sixty smaller islands. The main island is about twenty-six miles wide and stretches around fourteen miles from north to south.

Because it was formerly a British colony, it is a unique and interesting blend of the East and West. It is a collage of many cultures and people of many different ethnicities and beliefs peacefully coexisting. The population of five million people consists of around 75 percent Chinese, 13 percent Malay, and 9 percent Indian, and the remaining 3 percent are Eurasian. This diversity is reflected in the countries four official languages—English, Mandarin, Malay, and Tamil. After a while we learned that most everyone in Singapore speaks at least two languages fluently, and many speak three or four.

We soon realized that they also predominantly spoke their very own version of Singaporean English, which was nicknamed *Singlish*. In speaking with the local islanders, we could usually understand what they meant, although it was an original blend of broken British English and unique phrases. For instance, upon meeting them, they would always ask, "Have you taken your lunch yet?" This meant, "How are you?" It took me a few weeks to figure this out. I wondered why, regardless of what time of day it was, people asked me if I had already eaten lunch, even if it was five o'clock in the afternoon?

As it is located just three degrees from the equator, the squelching heat and high humidity struck me immediately while I was coming out of the airport for the first time. I felt like I was walking into a convection oven, and I began to sweat. This is how it would be almost every day of the next five years that we lived there. The sun rose at 7:00 a.m. and set at 7:00 p.m. every day with only a few minutes in variation. It usually cooled off a little after the sun set.

I have many wonderful memories of our life together in Singapore. Michael was initially more relaxed there. Being a part of Michael's world was often amazing. He attracted fascinating people and events to himself, and he knew how to live life well. He reveled in the finer things in life and was never afraid to ask for or reach for what he wanted. Having been his wife for so many years, I am grateful to have had the opportunity to enjoy these things with him. These wonderful things helped to balance out the difficulties of being married to an extremely powerful man who was very dedicated to his company.

We enjoyed many romantic evenings together surrounded by the tropical island splendor. We explored the bustling sophisticated city and tried new and exotic cuisine on the weekend evenings at restaurants located all over the island. There were plenty of interesting attractions and fun things to do. For some, living on an island would quickly become boring, but we had just moved from a small village in Germany to a metropolis full of entertainment and great live music being performed in many locations, so to me it felt similar to being back in civilization again.

We were happy to welcome many friends who visited from Germany as well as a few from my family. Before we left Germany, we had a big going-away party where Michael gave an unexpected open invitation for everyone to visit. And many of them welcomed the invitation. We had more than thirty visitors from Germany while we were living in Singapore. Some of them stayed for several weeks, and a few stayed for a number of months. So it often felt like I was managing a bed and breakfast. I usually didn't mind, as most of the time it was nice to have company.

As both of us enjoyed entertaining, there were many times throughout our marriage that I prepared a buffet dinner for fifty or more guests. Our home was often filled with interesting people from all over Asia and other parts of the world. I was able to prepare food for so many because of the early training I received from my mom and the minor degree I had in hotel and restaurant management.

Even my parents came to visit us. It appeared as though they were on their second honeymoon. I really admired their spirit! Although they were both over seventy years old, they did not allow the tropical heat to bother them one bit and they never complained once. They appeared to enjoy and soak up every morsel of adventure possible, and we tried to accommodate them as best we could. They sampled deliciously prepared dim sum at one of the finest restaurants in Singapore. And it was delightful to see them strolling hand in hand on the beach on the east coast, stopping to savor fresh coconut juice and sampling their first mango. Knowing how hard they had worked their entire lives and how stressful times had sometimes been in earlier days, it was fantastic to see them relaxing and enjoying themselves.

We had the opportunity of attending a traditional Hindu wedding with them. They were interested and open-minded, and they really enjoyed it. Two of Michael's school friends married Indian women from Singapore. We were asked to be the legal witnesses for one of their marriages, and from that time on her very large extended family invited us to many of their family celebrations. We have many pictures of our small daughter in the traditional Indian dress with the decorative red dot, called a *bindi,* on her forehead. I think my dad possibly felt like one of his favorite editions of *National Geographic* had come to life with so many nationalities and cultures represented in Singapore. When my dad passed away in 2010, my sister-in-law had the great idea of composing a booklet where my mom, each child, and grandchild wrote about their favorite memories with my dad. My mom wrote in his memorial booklet how their trip to Singapore was one of the best memories she had with my dad. This made me happy, as we had tried our best to spoil them while they were there as we realized how much they deserved it. Her positive memories also greatly encouraged me because some of my memories had been recently tinged in black when I discovered negative events that occurred while we lived there.

The ten years we lived in Asia were especially filled with extreme contrasts. For example, upon arriving in Singapore, I felt very privileged to spend our first days at the luxurious Shangri-La Hotel. It was because of Michael's success and hard work that we were able to stay there, as it was at his company's expense. Because of my modest upbringing and how I was raised, I don't feel that I ever took this for granted and even appreciated it more than the average person. We were treated exceptionally well. I often felt as though wherever we went in Asia we were treated similar to royalty because of Michael's position and strong self-confidence. It was sometimes baffling to me.

However, in contradiction, the very next day after we were graciously welcomed at the nice hotel, as I opened the door for the first time to what would be our new home, a big nest of giant flying cockroaches landed on my head. They had built a nest directly above the front door. I had never seen a cockroach before, let alone one that was three inches long. They had left a mess everywhere. I spent a day with rubber gloves and a strong disinfectant cleaning out the entire apartment. I feel that this example summarizes well how the next nine years in Asia would be.

Our first home in Singapore was in a gated community of 615 condominiums called Orchid Park. We lived on the seventh story, and there was a beautiful view overlooking the Seletar Reservoir. We could also see many palm trees and orchids in the tropical gardens below as well as a large fantastic swimming pool surrounded by lush greenery. As one entire wall of our condominium was made out of glass, it was particularly impressive to see the typhoons as they raced over the large reservoir toward us. As a fast-moving storm built up almost daily during the rainy season from November to February, the panoramic view of the sky was illuminated with bolts of lightning as they flashed across the entire atmosphere. I had never seen storms like this before, but I was not frightened, as I knew there were no tornadoes there.

That first afternoon I realized that our kitchen stove had no oven but only burners on the top. The local people did not bake, so it was not necessary to have one. Most people went out to eat every meal at the local food stalls on the ground floors of the massive apartment buildings. Moreover, our washing machine, which was outside on the balcony, had no hot water. Although I realized that I was more fortunate than most of those living in Southeast Asia, this meant that I would have to heat any hot water I needed on the stove and then carry it to the machine. In addition, the first morning I came in the kitchen to find the floor covered with large biting red ants.

That first night while I was attempting to sleep, I kept hearing a loud, constant, and unfamiliar chirping noise coming from the living room. It was much louder than a cricket or a frog, but I could not find anything. Finally I realized it was coming from underneath the TV stand. I got a flashlight and discovered a gecko that was hanging upside down under the TV stand. The noise was vibrating off of the bare granite floor of the fairly empty apartment, and that's why it was so loud. Although we lived on the seventh story, we discovered that geckos, giant flying cockroaches, as well as other insects had no problem finding their way in. I did not mind the geckos as much as the insects.

We had been there less than one year when Michael was asked to be responsible for the subsidiary and terminate the positions of the current managing director, his son, and many others because of corruption and embezzlement. It was exactly when he took over the company that I felt our lives change. This was when I felt a darkness descend upon us. To me, it felt real, and it was palpable. It was unlike anything I had ever experienced before. This was one week before the birth of our daughter.

One unusual incident happened just a few days later on the Sunday afternoon before she was born. We went for a brisk walk in hopes of encouraging her birth. I had been walking normally, and I suddenly went flying and landed right on my pregnant belly. I barely touched the ground and bounced right back up onto my feet. I felt as though I was lifted up by someone from underneath my arms and was briefly flying. It was very strange, and it felt surreal. Afterward, Michael and I both looked at each other in bewilderment. I believe neither of us was exactly sure what had just happened. I went to the doctor to make sure that the baby was fine, and she was. I did not have a scratch anywhere. I wish that we had had cameras on our cell phones back then and that Michael had filmed me, as I would be curious to see this myself. This experience was especially strange because I felt as though I had been pushed by someone and did not think that I had stumbled on a rock or anything else.

With tremendous joy, our daughter, Marie Christine, was born two days later on Tuesday, August 27, 1996. I had a pleasant and joyful pregnancy without any complications. Childbirth went very well until the very end, when I developed a serious life-threatening staph infection. When she was born, they initially could not get her to cry. Fortunately after they worked on her a while and suctioned her airways, she could breathe. Immediately following her birth I had a fever of over 104 degrees. It was so high that I was convulsing and my body was violently shaking as the infection surged through my blood. The fever was brought under control with intravenous antibiotics. Michael must not have realized the severity of it or how frightened I was, as he left us alone in a foreign country only a few minutes after my body stopped shaking uncontrollably. He had been there the entire day with me, and he was tired. I felt completely abandoned. From that time on his mind seemed to be completely focused on work and his new responsibilities in his new position as the managing director of Southeast Asia.

Upon returning home with a new baby I immediately became the secretary of this new company, answering the constantly ringing fax machine and phone in our small apartment. Despite my consulting several midwives, Marie was awake almost all night every night for many months, and she would first fall asleep at dawn. When she would occasionally start to fall asleep prior to this, she often screamed and seemed to be in pain, but the pediatrician could not find anything wrong with her. It seemed the second Michael walked out the door at 7:30 a.m. to go to work, Marie would wake up as the phone and fax machine would begin ringing with calls from other parts of the world. We had literally just fallen asleep. After several months of this I was completely exhausted.

In the weeks following her birth, all of Michael's colleagues from work and my friends from church presented us with small golden rats in the form of a pendant, necklace, or charm for a bracelet. I thought it was possibly a bad joke that I didn't get. I have never been fond of rats, but after my camp incident I strongly disliked them. Shortly thereafter I learned that it was "the year of the rat" in Chinese astrology, and these gifts were considered to be very auspicious.

The staph infection I contracted in the hospital kept resurfacing in different parts of my body and in my blood. It seemed that after six weeks of being treated with antibiotics, our immune systems were compromised. Regretfully Marie received the same antibiotics as I did through my breast milk. In 1996, there was much less knowledge about the benefits of probiotics to protect and strengthen immunity. A few months later Marie and I were in an almost constant cycle of bronchitis and more antibiotics.

Fortunately there was a nice doctor within walking distance that Michael nicknamed "Doctor Elvis." He was very gracious, spoke English well, and looked like a Chinese Elvis impersonator, sideburns and all.

What may have also contributed to our almost constant bronchitis was that there were several months in 1997 when we did not see the sky in Singapore, as thick black smog filled the air. They called it "the Haze," and it was a large-scale air-quality disaster affecting much of Southeast Asia. Some of it was from illegal crop burning in nearby Indonesia. We were warned to stay inside as much as possible and advised to wear masks if we needed to go outside.

On a much happier note Marie was a complete joy to be with. She is the greatest gift I have ever been given. She was happy, bright, funny, and smart and seemed to spread that happiness to everyone wherever we went. She seemed to be born wise beyond her years and many people would comment on this. She loved to be with people and to see new things. She was smiling most of the time, and her giggle was infectious.

Whenever I could, I took her out for daily walks in her buggy. Most of the other Americans and Europeans lived in an area called Holland Village, which was near the main street and shopping district on Orchard Road. Because we lived in a more affordable area in the northern part of the island, we lived amongst several British and Australian families and many Singaporeans.

I remember one morning when Marie could first crawl but could not yet speak. It was shortly after 9:00 a.m., and we hadn't yet been out of the house. She came crawling toward me, dragging her buggy with one hand and my shoes in the other. She held my shoes up to me as if to say, "Come on. Let's go!" So we went!

Finding a nice place to walk nearby was challenging not only because of the tropical heat but also because of the many creatures that inhabited the island. I first went with her to an area near the Seletar Reservoir that looked nice. I was stopped by someone who told me that it was too dangerous, as there were baby crocodiles that time of year. I thought, *If there are babies, are there also mommy crocodiles?* I wondered why there wasn't a sign posted. There might have been one in Chinese or Malay, neither of which I could read. Then we went to a park about half a mile from our home where I walked often during my pregnancy. A local woman stopped me. She said, "Lady, you cannot walk here with a baby. A snake could crawl into the buggy and bite your baby! You can only walk here if you have a snakebite kit with you. Do you have a snakebite kit with you?"

After this we limited our walks mostly to the nearby Chinese market. Marie liked that much more anyway, as she was able to see a lot of people. As we went through the small streets lined with exotic foods, it took some tolerance and getting used to, as many of the food items for sale turned my stomach. The local people always seemed to be happy to see us coming. Marie would often be waving before we even got there, and they would wave back at her from a distance. When she was a baby, she had lots of curly strawberry blonde hair. By the age of two and a half, she had beautiful long golden blonde hair, so it was easy to recognize her amidst a nation of black-haired individuals. I think because she was so happy and friendly, everywhere we went in Asia, people would ask if they could take their picture with her. She has seen many airplane cockpits and restaurant kitchens, as people would often ask if they could pick her up and carry her around. She often emerged with a treat of some kind. Because of this, Michael thought she was destined from a young age to be an ambassador.

We often took the train into the city, where we would explore one of the many shopping centers. The train was very comfortable and safe. A nice shopping mall was a huge treat, as there were no shopping malls in Germany at that time except in the larger cities. We also went almost every week to the zoo, which was always great. We have photos of us at the zoo with orangutans, monkeys, and macaws.

Only 15 percent of Singaporeans own cars, as they are very expensive. The government places a tax of at least 100 percent on the vehicle in addition to a large fee for the title of owning a car. Therefore, we could not afford a car. Michael had a company car, but I did not drive it for several months because it was intimidating knowing the price of the vehicle. In addition, as it was formerly a British colony, they drive as people do in Great Britain on the opposite side of the road. When holding a baby and bags of groceries for hours while waiting for a taxi in the sweltering heat became increasingly inconvenient, I learned to drive Michael's company car. He was not using it much of the time anyway as he was traveling. I started out small, driving to get groceries and to church, which were both one mile from our home. Very soon I was driving all over the island, and it became an almost weekly ritual for Marie and I to drop off and pick up Michael at the airport.

In 1998, we moved into a newly developed gated community that was in Northern Singapore called Lentor Villas. It was near the Malaysian border. We were the first ones to move into the entire complex of 182 terraced houses. Although the house was very nice and had beautiful floors and a lovely wooden staircase, I had an inexplicable uneasy feeling when we viewed it for the first time, and I did not want to move there. Michael really liked it and wanted to move there as soon as possible, so we did. Several weeks before we moved in, we shipped all of our possessions over from our apartment in Germany.

While I was unpacking the first box a few minutes after we had moved in, a very large yellow snake slithered out of the closet on the main floor near the front door. It was about six inches in diameter and at least eight feet long, so it moved quite fast like a wave. I had never seen a snake that big before except in a zoo. It looked like a python, but I do not know what kind it was for sure. I quickly ran out the back door with Marie. I was used to and even liked garter snakes as a kid, but this was not a garter snake. Luckily the security guard from the front gate was nearby, and he called to get someone to remove it. They said it must have come in from the jungle in back of our house. We soon realized that in the evening, we could hear many unfamiliar exotic animal and bird noises coming from the jungle right behind our house.

I encountered one other creature when Marie and I were walking hand in hand down the long wooden staircase on her third birthday. I was anxious to bring her to the traditional birthday table, where her gifts and cards were waiting for her to open. She said excitedly, "Look, Mommy.

Spider!" She pointed up toward the wall above us. I looked up, and about four feet above us was what looked like a tarantula. It was as big as my spread hand. I now feel badly that I killed a living creature; however, I acted on instinct, and I did not want this spider to surprise or bite us at a later time, perhaps when we were sleeping. I got Marie to safety, threw a wet bundled up rag at the spider, sprayed it with bug spray when it fell to the ground, and then used a fly swatter to kill it. Seeing these same monstrous spiders hanging on the window screens became normal when we later lived in Japan.

As we were the very first family to move in, it looked like a ghost town during the first months, as it was otherwise completely deserted. It slowly became occupied with families from all over the world. I like to organize events and meet new people, so I planned neighborhood picnics and festivities for us to get to know one another. This was a lot of fun, and our new neighbors enthusiastically participated.

Marie and I went swimming daily at the pool, where we met other moms and kids from many different countries. We also took early evening walks and bike rides around the large complex almost daily when the heat resided. We were often invited into various homes to join families from many nationalities for conversation and a karaoke session. I have spent time singing with practicing Muslims, Hindus, Buddhists, and people of many nationalities from numerous parts of the world. As karaoke was very popular in Asia at that time, we were invited into many Singaporean homes. It was surprising, as many local people had almost no furniture, except what one needed for karaoke—a couch, a great hi-fi system, and at least two high-quality microphones. Most of the families living there were mixed nationalities, so we had this common bond. Many had also traveled a lot or were away from their families and home countries, so they were generally very open and friendly. What I realized during these singing sessions was that we are all much more alike than we are different. We all have the same needs. It's just that a few extreme people ruin it for many people.

Unfortunately it was also after we moved into this house that we started experiencing paranormal activity. It began with the feeling of fear or evil that was accompanied by a black mist, sometimes in the shape of men, clouds, or what one would call *ghosts*. This was the first time I had ever felt and seen tangible evil before.

In addition, objects began falling down on top of us. I also started falling down a lot and usually landed on my knees. I often felt as though I had been pushed by a strong, unexplained, invisible force. From the time I felt this evil, I also had increased hunger, which was frustrating. I felt like I was starving much of the time, and I started to gain weight. I believe I was in an almost constant fight-or-flight response from this time on.

Michael did not ever mention feeling this uncomfortable and evil feeling, but it seemed to be affecting him in other ways. I knew that Marie did, as she would often wake up, become afraid, and begin to scream or cry. It was a different type of crying than normal, as if she was in pain. As she got older, she began to express that she was seeing the same images as I was, whether they were in the form of what she called black witches or ghosts that were chasing her.

One of these events happened when Marie was three years old. She was playing in the room next to the kitchen, and I was about six feet away from her. At that time we had a standing wardrobe from Germany in her playroom, and it was about eight feet tall by nine feet long. Very suddenly a big heavy door became unhinged with absolutely no visible warning, and it was headed to land right on top of her. Without even a second of hesitation, she stretched out her arms above her head and caught the door. She said with delight, "Look, Mommy. I caught it!" She was not frightened or visibly shaken. It was a truly unbelievable site. I just kept saying what my mom had always said, "Thank you, God. Thank you, Jesus. Thank you, angels." Our days and nights became littered with abnormal, frightening, and uncomfortable events.

Still to this day I do not know how she so often caught falling objects. In Asia, it seemed there was constant movement and construction almost everywhere we went. I could only occasionally block out the everyday sound of jackhammers. One day we were in a newly built shopping center, and a huge, heavy, cast-iron standing wall fell over and landed right on top of us. I tried my best to protect Marie. We were both knocked to the ground, but I caught it enough that it did not hurt us at all, except for the impact of hitting the ground. I don't believe I could have ever held up that heavy wall by myself. This time, we were both shaken and crying. This was partially because I was so discouraged feeling as though there was some unexplained invisible force at work in our lives and I felt helpless.

When some men rushed to our assistance, I couldn't begin to lift it off of us on my own at all. My only explanation was that once again we had help from our angels, and I felt that despite everything that was occurring, someone from above was protecting us. I was grateful and kept thanking them.

Singapore is one of the safest countries in the world because of their tough crime laws, which are rigidly enforced. They still had public hangings every Friday, and the pictures and names of the men who were to be hanged were made public in the newspaper every week. Most of them were arrested for drug trafficking.

The fear I felt in the house at night grew and intensified. In addition, I often felt that there were men in the jungle behind our house. In my mind I could see three of them. This frustrated me, as I did not want to let my imagination cause me unnecessary fear and keep me awake with worry. At that time I did not know if this was only in my imagination or a real warning sign. I knew it was not completely inconceivable because I often saw men climbing the fence into the jungle right next to our home because there were several trees with the prized jackfruit growing there. One evening we arrived home to find police cars surrounding our house and the entire neighborhood. We had been in Thailand for a long weekend because Michael wanted to celebrate his birthday there.

The police were there because three men had broken into the house two down from ours and had taken their little girl at knifepoint into the jungle directly behind our houses, demanding ransom money for the girl. They believed these men had possibly come by boat from nearby Indonesia. I could not help but wonder how it might have been us if we had been home.

The police camped out in the third story of the two unoccupied houses directly next to ours for a few weeks, as they were waiting for these men to return. The men fled deeper into the jungle, and the officers felt that they might still be hiding there. Although the presence of the police keeping watch from the empty houses directly next to ours on both sides was somewhat comforting, the fact that we needed undercover police concerned me. Furthermore, it did not help me to know that my intuition had been right in feeling and seeing that there were men in the jungle behind our house. After this we placed an iron door on the entrance of our bedroom that resembled a prison cell door and we also installed an alarm system.

Every time I moved to a new city or country, I always found my church community first and then joined the choir. Almost instantly I would have twenty or thirty new friends and my new church would become my second home. My voice has always been a tremendous gift to me in this way, and I have been singing at church since I was about ten or twelve years old. I always felt a great connection to God and my spirit while I was singing. I especially appreciate that my parents always supported my singing and they never once asked me to be silent, but instead asked me to keep singing and to sing louder. In Singapore, the church became my second home as well. In addition to Sunday Mass, I attended the weekly Wednesday night healing service, which was part of the Catholic Charismatic Renewal.

At Our Lady, Star of the Sea, I was the only white woman in the entire congregation. I soon developed several close friendships within the healing prayer group. I had often attended this type of healing service with my mom when I was a teenager. It consists of praise and worship, praying, inviting the Holy Spirit to come, prophetic words being spoken, the baptism of the Holy Spirit, the impartation of gifts from the Holy Spirit, and speaking in tongues. It was during this time that I first experienced words coming out of my mouth, as if I had no control. "I am the way, the truth and the life. No one comes to the Father except through me." I kept seeing Jesus, and he was speaking this through me.

This was possibly because most of these parishioners were new and first-generation believers in God and Jesus. I got to know many former Buddhists well during the nine years that I lived in Asia, and several of them told me that they had never prayed to this God, whom they now felt like they knew. They had formerly only prayed for gold (money), good luck, and fortune. I am certain this is not true for all Buddhists, but this is what my formerly Buddhist friends shared with me. I also spent time with many former Hindus who said that they prayed to many deities but never felt like they knew this one God until they became Christians. Again I don't believe that this is true for all Hindus, but this was what my formerly Hindu friends expressed to me.

I felt very much at home there, and they made me feel very welcome. For many of them it was the first time that they had ever met a white woman from the West. As I was one of the only ones in the entire parish of hundreds that could bake, I baked dozens of half-sized cakes and muffins in my small countertop oven for various events at the church. They were thankful, and it was hard for them to believe that I could do this. For me this was just normal.

In addition, I joined a class on transcendental meditation that was approved by and offered at the church. It has been proven that if practiced correctly, one can reach a deeper state of relaxation than the deepest sleep provides, therefore causing great health benefits of increased serotonin levels and decreased cortisol. I practiced this for about a year. I found that I was able to easily relax deeply, and it was simple. There are many health benefits to calming the mind and body and one heightens the possibility of connecting with the inner consciousness and God.

I attended the Wednesday night healing service every week since our arrival in Singapore in September of 1995. On December 6, 1995, during the healing portion of the Mass, I requested that the prayer group pray over me that we would conceive a baby. Miraculously, two days later, on the anniversary of the day we met, we did! On December 26, I had the wonderful news that I was pregnant. So in my eyes Marie is a miracle in more than one way. This remarkable experience reconfirmed and strengthened my belief in prayer and miracles.

My friends from church called Marie the "charismatic baby." I think because she was the only baby who came to the service every week and because they knew they had prayed over me to conceive her. Toward the end of each service the priest usually prays over everyone who wishes to receive healing, and some people "rest in the spirit." This is when the Holy Spirit fills a person with a heightened inner awareness of his presence, and the body can no longer stand, and usually one collapses to the ground. The person remains conscious but is under the healing power of the Holy Spirit. This was for me one of the most loving, comforting, and blissful experiences I had ever had in my life. I am not exactly sure why, but just like when I attended these services when I was a teenager, whenever the priest came near me, I would uncontrollably collapse to the floor in a blissful state. There are usually two or more stronger men who act as *catchers* at these services for anyone who needs them.

One evening in one of the normally peaceful services, an extremely loud and horrible voice started speaking. It was coming out of a petite Indian woman I was acquainted with. The voice was so loud and deep and dark that it sounded as though it could not be coming out of any human being. Her body was shaking and reeling. The whole church remained still, except for a few men who ran to assist the priest while he performed an exorcism right there in front of everyone. I wondered if anyone was as horrified as I by what was happening. It appeared as though this did not shock or surprise the locals. It was as if it was not the first time they had seen this.

Two weeks later the same Indian woman attended the healing service. She appeared to be fine and was in good spirits. She walked directly toward me after the service and started telling me all about what she was experiencing and feeling during the exorcism. I thought, *Why are you telling me this?* It frightened me, and I did not want to hear about it. She kept talking and even followed me out to my car as I tried to politely leave. Then she even entered my car on the passenger side as I tried to escape into the drivers seat. She proceeded to tell me that her sister-in-law had cursed her because she was angry with her, and very quickly all of her major organs began to shut down. She said that her husband had brought her from the hospital, where she was dying, to the healing service that night. She had been instantly healed following the intervention from the priest. This was the first time I had witnessed an instant miraculous healing, and at the same time I had seen and heard something that scared me so much.

Later when I was speaking with my Singaporean friends, I found out that they all knew and accepted that these things existed and were a part of their culture. They expressed how they thought that they were given special protection against evil and curses when they came to the healing service. One of them told me that they were aware that in the West we do not want to believe that these things really exist, whereas these relatively new Christians all knew and believed that evil existed. This experience changed me in that I witnessed something evil physically manifest in a woman that I was acquainted with, and I saw the power of Jesus drive it out of her and instantly and miraculously heal her.

Tranquility

After five years in Singapore we moved to Japan for two years beginning in January of 2000. Once again Michael was asked to set up a new subsidiary there for his company in Germany. He had set up many subsidiaries all over Asia while we were living in Singapore, and he was very talented and efficient at this. Although I was raised with very hardworking men and women and my former boss had also accused me of being a workaholic, he was driven beyond anyone I had ever known. It did not seem natural.

From the first day we arrived in Yokohama, I had the feeling that I would be happy there, and I was. The energy felt very positive and much more peaceful than it felt in Singapore. For the most part it was a phenomenal experience.

We found a nice home and a wonderful school for Marie on what is called "the Bluff" area of Yokohama. We lived on the top two floors of the house, and a nice Australian family with three small children lived on the first floor. Directly across from our house was a beautiful park filled with rose gardens overlooking the impressive Yokohama Harbor. Anyone who knows me well knows that I love all kinds of roses. There were also many cherry trees in this large park. Seeing the blossoming cherry trees (*sakura*) in Japan in the spring remains one of my favorite memories during our nine years in Asia. I walked there almost every day with Marie after school. It was very serene. I felt and saw no evil the entire time we lived in Japan, and we also were not sick. Although this was a huge relief, it was at the same time puzzling. It seemed to confirm my suspicions that we were not really physically ill, and there was some strange invisible force from the outside causing the sickness and paranormal activity.

Through the school I met wonderful friends from the United States as well as many other countries. I found the Japanese people to be extremely gracious, peaceful, and honorable. I was happily busy serving as class mom and volunteering at the school and various local charities. The other American class mom and I organized some great day trips by train to some very interesting and beautiful places in Japan. The word spread from expat to expat about where the nicest places were to visit. There was an American club that offered great activities for both Marie and me. I met several really nice moms from the Philippines, and we had a fun karaoke session over lunch once a month. Once again I found an excellent church community, and after a short while I began singing there on a weekly basis and made nice friends in the choir. It was composed of local Japanese people as well as expats from many countries. It was great, as there was a terrific sense of community there, and I felt as at home as one can feel in a foreign country.

The most uncomfortable thing about living there was that there were some months when we experienced almost daily earthquakes. This took some getting used to, but our home and most of the newer buildings were built to withstand them. We just happened to be living there on the seventy-seventh anniversary of the Great Kanto Earthquake, and there was quite a bit of superstitious talk regarding another big one occurring around the seventy-eighth year. In order to have peace of mind, I decided I just had to put it out of my mind, which was sometimes a little difficult when the entire house was swaying back and forth.

Michael was very busy setting up another company and establishing more connections in Asia. He attracted so many interesting people and events into our lives that there was never a dull moment. He gravitated toward the finest hotels and restaurants in every city he visited. It was not unusual for him to ask me on the phone, "You'll never guess who I saw in the restaurant in the hotel where I was tonight?" His answer was sometimes well-known people like Hillary Clinton or David Beckham.

One time Marie's very pleasant Japanese preschool teacher's assistant thought she should bring it to my attention that Marie often told very imaginative stories at school. She said, "Marie told me today that her daddy had dinner last night with the president of Indonesia."

I replied, "Yes, he did have dinner with him last night, but now he is the former president." I don't think that was the response she had expected. Often we didn't realize Marie was even paying attention to our conversations, but as time went on, it was evident that she didn't miss a thing. I understood that many of the stories she possibly told sounded unbelievable, as they did to me as well.

During the two years in Japan we had one particularly peculiar incident. One Friday morning I was at a school meeting with my American friend Janice. After the meeting she said out of the blue, "If you ever see one of those giant centipedes, you should be careful, as they can be poisonous and you need to go immediately to the emergency room for an antivenin treatment." She and her daughter had just learned about them at a Girl Scout meeting, and I could tell it had upset her a little. I thought, *Hmm. Okay?* I didn't really think much about it, as I didn't think I would actually ever see one.

On the following Sunday I woke up and told my husband that I had the feeling that we should find where the nearest emergency room was just in case we ever needed one. Thankfully he went along with it. I did not understand why, but I had a strong nudging to find one.

That same night I got up around 3:00 a.m. to switch on the air conditioner and felt something wiggling under my foot. It then whipped up and bit my ankle, and it was hissing quite loudly. I had never heard hissing like this before. I turned on the light and saw that it was a thick brown centipede about five inches long. Something told me to catch him, so I quickly put a nearby decorative dish over him. I woke up Michael, and I told him that a big centipede had just bitten me. Understandably he did not believe me and asked me to go back to sleep, as he thought I must have dreamt it. I quickly got some bug spray, tongs, and a plastic bag. After I sprayed it, I put the centipede in the bag and showed it to him. He also had never seen one of them before. He got up right away and drove me to the emergency room.

As I could not speak much Japanese and did not know the word for centipede, I listened to my intuition and brought the plastic bag with me. When I arrived, I simply had to hold up the bag with the squirming centipede in it, and the doctor and nurse said very loudly and simultaneously, "Mukade!" The doctor instantly began an infusion. After about an hour I was able to return home that night with my family with the understanding that I return at 8:00 a.m. the next morning for an evaluation. We all slept together in our living room on one big sofa that transformed into a bed. I kept one eye open!

The next day it seemed like a plague of these insects were pouring into our house from somewhere. At one point I looked toward the end of the long entrance hallway and saw at least fifty of them scampering toward me like mice. I will never forget it! I later learned that they are attracted to body heat and weren't purposely trying to catch me as it first appeared. After the initial disbelief wore off, I did my best to capture them while keeping a safe distance. Later while I was showering, I looked down and saw that they were swimming in the water at the bottom of the tub. So I think they were coming in through the water system. That was the quickest shower I ever had in my life.

I called the landlord, but he did not believe me. He would not come, and he did not call an exterminator. I contacted the head of entomology from the University of Kansas and asked for advice. I began killing them with wasp spray, which I did not like to use. I used tongs and placed them in a big glass jar. I collected about fifty of them and brought them to our landlord. He could not believe it. He said in his broken English, "It cannot be."

I replied, "But it is!"

We slept with Marie in between us in our king-sized bed with two thick layers of double-sided tape on the carpeting all around the perimeter of our bed. I changed this tape every day and caught several smaller ones on the sticky tape. One morning I woke up and felt something in my hair. I quickly bent over and shook out my hair, and sure enough, a three-inch centipede fell to the floor. Fortunately I was not bitten. I am not sure why we did not move into a hotel. I think we probably stayed because it would have been very expensive and inconvenient to go to a hotel, and we did not know that there would be so many of them and that it would go on for so long. It was eventually settled weeks later with the help of an exterminator.

It was possible that these insects had been living in the ground that had recently been dug up for a house that was newly built next to the house we were living in. It appeared as though this land had never been disturbed before. It was also possible that they had been living in a large pile of newspapers that was stored in a small room in our garage and removed shortly before this time. When we moved in, the newspapers looked as though they had been there a long time, and it was damp and humid in the garage, which was the perfect environment for these insects.

Although it was upsetting to have large poisonous insects in our house, we finally understood one thing. Every time we went shopping for groceries during the five years that we lived in Singapore, we walked by a display at a hardware store that was an advertisement for a chemical used to treat home water systems. This display consisted of a large transparent water pipe that was connected to a bathtub and a sink. The water pipe was filled with flowing water in which there were big plastic centipedes as well as other over-sized plastic insects. We used to chuckle at it and think how fake it was. We thought, *Why would there ever be huge insects like that in your water system?* And now we finally understood it and wished that we had some of this chemical.

Marie and I in Tokyo

The Dark Night of the Soul

W e moved back to Germany in 2002 and into a third-story apartment in a village called Niedernhall, which was just two kilometers from Michael's hometown. This village is more than 750 years old. The sizable building that we moved into had a rich history and had formerly housed a blacksmith many years prior. The first floor was occupied by a company and was converted into an office. There were two apartments, each on the second and third stories. A married couple, both architects, had previously lived in the two third-story apartments with their three small children. They had renovated it and created a beautiful open living area with large windows overlooking the small village, impressive valley, and lovely vineyards. The view was really nice, and we especially enjoyed a spacious open balcony. There was a little girl Marie's age that lived in the apartment below us, and they became instant friends and played together daily.

The biggest disadvantage was that there was no elevator, and so we had to carry all of the groceries and anything we needed up the three stories of stairs. This was normal in a country where practicality usually precedes convenience. In Germany at this time glass was used instead of plastic recyclables, so there were usually many heavy items to carry. In addition, we were living directly under the roof, which would be comparable to living in the attic in a home in the United States, and there is very rarely air-conditioning in private homes in Germany, so it was extremely hot and uncomfortable in the summer months.

It was at this time that this mysterious illness returned and became much worse. I had a constant fever, extreme pressure and what sounded like a constant roaring ocean in my head, abnormal hunger, and a ringing in my ears. I experienced almost constant pain all over shoulders and head, and my energy felt completely drained. I often had bronchitis, pneumonia, or a throat infection. Marie also often had a fever and bronchitis. The feeling of something evil being over us was stronger than it was in Singapore, and it kept me awake almost all night every night. Possibly one of the worst things was that when I would finally be able to sleep, I would often wake up in a panic and feel like someone was choking me or like I was suffocating and couldn't breathe. I would quickly sit up in my bed and call out the name of Jesus. There were many times I was very concerned that I would not recover my ability to breathe. It was very alarming and extremely frightening. I could not understand this at all. It was not like me to have what seemed like recurring panic attacks while sleeping.

I felt like I was in a spiritual battle with an invisible enemy. I kept asking God to show me who or what I was battling against. I was in bed with a crucifix on one side, a Bible on the other, several scapulars on, and holy water next to me. All I could do was pray. I prayed the rosary daily and several novenas to St. Jude and the holy family, and I found great comfort in reading the Bible. I began to read the Bible out loud and practiced taking my authority as a child of God, putting on the full armor of God, as in Ephesians 6:11, and using the blood of Jesus for protection. When I could, I would sing and praise God.

Although I had listened to the gospel readings at church throughout my entire life and had sung the psalms on a regular basis, I had never read the Bible in its entirety before. During this time I read it all the way through more than once. It comforted me. It seemed the more I spoke the word of God out loud, the more strength I found and the more I was able to sleep. Sometimes I would ask the Holy Spirit to guide me as to what I should read. The book of Tobit and the story of Archangel Raphael kept surfacing repeatedly, and I did not understand why. I already had a strong devotion to St. Michael (or Archangel Michael) since I was very young, not even knowing exactly why, except that he was the protector of the church and against evil. I knew that I felt comforted when I prayed for him to be with me. But I did not know much about Raphael before this time.

Another coincidence regarding Archangel Raphael was that around this exact time my sister made a decision to leave her profession as a doctor of infectious diseases and become a nun with the Sisters of Life in the Bronx, New York. She chose the name Sr. Johanna Raphael. This sparked my interest even more in Raphael, and I wanted to know more about him. I knew that she had a connection with him and she and I are very close. What I also found interesting is that my mom and dad almost named her Johanna when she was born but instead named her Judy. I had never heard this before until she chose that name, and then my mom told me. I do not know if my sister knew, or if this was just a coincidence.

Throughout these months many mornings I got up feeling like I was a dog that had been beaten all night long. I had a fever, very little energy, and I was in pain, especially on my neck, back, shoulders, and head. I remember praying for just one day of relief from the pressure in my head as it sometimes felt as if it was going to explode. As humor has often helped me cope in difficult times, I wearily joked with the local doctor that my daughter and I should rent a room at the clinic, as we were there so often. He looked at me with concern and did not laugh. I don't think he knew that I was trying to bring some humor into a depressing situation. I did feel his genuine desire to help us, and I appreciated it.

One time I was there for what was about the twentieth blood test, searching for some sort of infection that could possibly be causing the fever, pain, and exhaustion. I could hardly keep my eyes open and my head up. When he asked me about my symptoms, I mistakenly told him that I felt like I had been run over by a bicycle (*Farhrrad* in German). I meant to say *car* or *truck* (*Fahrzeug*). I was too tired at the time to recognize my mistake. Although he knew me well by now, I don't think he knew at all what I meant to say and just looked at me with confusion. It was only when I got home that I realized what I had said, and I had to laugh at myself.

During this time I had many medical tests both in the United States and in Germany. As always, every doctor concluded that I had a fever but could not find any reason for my illness. I was misdiagnosed several times, which caused me unnecessary worrying. One doctor, upon seeing a bulging left kidney after I had a kidney function radiology test using contrast dye, informed me that there was a tumor on my kidney. Upon more evaluation I was told that I had what is called a dromedary hump, which is a small bulge on the lateral border of the left kidney. It is a mass that simulates a tumor. I was temporarily very worried for nothing.

Because I knew a few Americans who had contracted tropical diseases and parasites while they were living in Asia, I also considered the possibility that we may have gotten some rare tropical disease and that this was the reason for the fever and illness. Therefore, my daughter and I were also examined at the Tropical Disease Institute at the University of Heidelberg in Germany. This ruled out any possible tropical disease that we might have contracted.

Whatever this fever was caused by, it was also resistant to antibiotics. By this time I was often too weak to drive. I missed singing in choir practice and visiting my friends. Many days I felt it was not safe for me to drive one mile, as my brain was in a fog and I felt confused. I felt like my life was passing me by. I did not tell most of my family, as I had no diagnosis and I didn't want to worry them. I only told my sister, who was a physician and was now a nun in the Bronx. I asked for the prayers of the nuns at the Sisters of Life and I believe these prayers really helped. I felt I could not explain it to my family or friends, as I could not understand it myself. At the same time I felt that we were not physically sick. This was verified to me by the completely healthy two years with no sense of evil while we lived in Japan. I felt strongly that it was something that did not belong to us.

Because smiling and laughing has always been a part of my nature, and I was raised to put my best foot forward and not to complain, I think, except for my closest friends, no one even knew that I was often sick. One major fault of mine is that I do not ever want to burden anyone when I have a problem. So I do not share it with anyone. I have recently learned that this is often a disservice to those I care about. Instead of me hiding everything and trying to do everything myself, I could have possibly allowed those close to me to help me and they would have been happy that I accepted their help and support. There is possibly also a small part of me that does want everyone to see as clearly as I do that I am not perfect.

I was in spiritual torment. To combat this, I said the rosary daily, the Chaplet of the Divine Mercy, and many other prayers. As Jesus has always been my number one, there were many times I felt as though I could feel him holding me. I could also imagine him sitting directly across from me and holding my hands. Sometimes I thought I really felt him comforting me, and then I knew that he was there. When I could, I would sing songs of praise and worship God in my kitchen.

During this entire time I also had a strong feeling that I was supposed to be doing something important, but I had no idea what. When I told this to Michael, he said, "Isn't it enough just to be my wife?" Of course it was. I loved being his wife and I considered it to be a privilege at the time, but despite how proud I was of him, this nagging, nudging feeling remained like a faded memory. So I kept asking God to show me what it was that he wanted me to be doing. Every day I would ask him to lead me and guide me to where he wanted me to be. I also kept asking him to show me why we were so sick and what this invisible enemy was. I truly felt like I was fighting for my life and the life of our daughter, not knowing how to fight this enemy or how to win this battle.

The Traumatic Brain Injury

September of 2003 began one of the darkest periods of my life. As we lived on the top floor of a large apartment building, we were directly under the roof, which was made of bricks and covered with a layer of cement. We had one small storage closet in the apartment that was directly under the slant of the roof. As the slant met the floor at a 45 degree angle, we always had to be careful not to bump our heads in these places. Michael was better at remembering this than I was, as he had grown up with these types of ceilings. For me this was the first time I had encountered them, and every time I went in the closet, I had to remind myself to be careful. One afternoon while I was not feeling well but was determined to exercise, I went into the cramped closet and tried to lift my heavy stationary exercise bike out into the living-room area. I accidentally dropped it, and the force of releasing it caused me to bump my head really hard on the brick ceiling. I became unusually sleepy after that. I remember lying down on the couch, and then I must have fallen asleep.

The next thing I remember, I woke up. I saw what looked like Satan himself and two horrific-looking beings walking together in our front door and straight into our living room. Their *arms* were interlocked. I screamed out of terror. I only saw them for a few seconds, but I felt the air pressure change and the temperature drop. I had never seen anything this frightening before. The blow to my head seemed to have temporarily opened up my spiritual vision. It was comparable to having a nightmare while I was fully awake.

That evening Michael was traveling as usual, and so Marie, who was seven years old at the time, was sleeping with me in our bed. I also kept her near me because of what I had seen walk through the front door earlier. I woke up around 3:30 a.m. to a pounding headache. I was extremely dizzy and nauseated, and the whole room was spinning. I felt as though I was paralyzed and had the weight of six big men sitting on top of me, pinning me down. I could hardly move my arms or speak. I managed to wake up Marie, who called 110, the German 911. Thankfully in Germany doctors still made house calls. He came within thirty minutes and examined me. He was very kind. He gave me an infusion, which suppressed the dizziness and nausea. After he asked me some questions, he also looked all around the apartment for any medicine or food that I might have ingested to cause this. At that time I remembered absolutely nothing about bumping my head that afternoon. He told me he would visit me again in the morning, and he arranged for medical tests the next day.

The next morning when we woke up, I was still very weak but felt less dizzy and queasy. However, Marie was covered from head to toe with chicken pox. More strangely Marie's two cute floppy-eared bunnies that were in the hallway right outside our front door were lying dead. It was so strange that I would hardly believe all of this myself if it hadn't happened to us and I didn't still have the photographs to prove it.

I had an appointment to have an MRI of my skull the next day at a large hospital one hour away. I also saw another doctor who examined my head, and I received an ultrasound and other tests to see if all of the veins and arteries leading to my head were healthy. Michael's mom drove me and watched Marie. As I was preparing to go and began to brush my hair, I felt a huge bump on my head, and it was extremely painful. It was only then that I remembered bumping my head on the brick/cement ceiling the afternoon before.

I had to wait a few days for the results of the MRI, which revealed a cerebral contusion or bruised brain from the blow to my head. He also said I had most likely experienced a severe concussion by the amount of swelling. The MRI also uncovered three small lesions in my brain. At first he thought they might possibly be tumors, but he ruled that out after more evaluation. He believed they were either from an old head trauma or that they might signal the beginning of MS. He recommended that I have another MRI in six months. I had been studying the Bible enough to know to reject the thought of MS immediately. I could not accept that. I sent the X-rays to my sister for her opinion. I also sent them to the radiologist at the hospital near my hometown for his opinion. He also believed the lesions were from an old head trauma. As temporarily scared as I was at the thought of having brain tumors, I was so tired of being sick that I almost welcomed any diagnosis just to know what it was so that I could begin to feel better.

About a week later I received a call from a different doctor who had examined and taken X-rays of my head and skull. His name was Dr. Christ. (Strange, huh?) He sounded very upset. He told me that I had many abrasions on my skull, and he asked me if I knew what they were from. I said that I didn't know. The only thing I could think of was that I fell down a couple of times when I roller-skated as a kid. He said, "No, that can't be it. There are too many markings, and they are too big and too deep. There had to have been a lot of force used." He told me that I had to find out what they were from. He seemed to be getting increasingly upset that I wasn't more concerned or that I wasn't taking him seriously enough. Because I have been through so much in my lifetime, I don't think I get upset quickly or easily. I know that everything is easier when I remain calm. As he got more upset, he talked faster. Although I still make grammatical errors when I am speaking and writing German, I can usually converse with anyone and understand what is being said. I wondered if there was something I didn't understand, so I asked him to speak with my friend Lori, who worked as a registered nurse for many years in Germany. Her German was better than mine, and her knowledge of medical terms in German exceeded mine. She understood him to be saying the exact same thing as I thought.

After this I was dizzy and weak for much of three months. I had additional new symptoms, such as an extreme sensitivity to light. Even candlelight was intolerable. Driving at night was impossible for several years as I became dizzy and was panic- stricken, not understanding why. Again I struggled through and tried my best to live as normal of a life as possible. It was not like me to be nervous or panic.

All this while I did have some good days, and I usually had a few good hours every afternoon when I would do my housework as fast as I could, pick Marie up from school, and spend time helping her with her homework. Because I was a fast worker and Michael traveled usually for two weeks at a time all over the world, I don't think he ever realized how sick I was. As long as the house was immaculate, his white dress shirts were laundered and pressed, and a nice dinner was promptly on the table when he arrived home, he didn't seem to notice. I felt as though he had begun to live a separate life without us when Marie was very young, and he was usually completely focused on his work or getting the next big sale for his company or a grander frequent flyer status. There were many years when we only saw him for a few hours every other Saturday evening. We spoke on the phone at least twice a day, and I received many loving text messages every day and beautiful bouquets of flowers frequently. Communication is his forte, and he told me every time we talked how much he loved me and thanked me for my fantastic support.

By this time I had heard of a few spiritual healers in our area, but I was afraid to go. I was not sure if it was wrong to see a healer. I had spoken to several priests over the years, but I could not find one that could help me. Two of them weren't even sure if evil existed. I was sure there must be someone who could help me, but I didn't know how to find him or her. I also often mistakenly thought I had to go through this alone.

My neighbor told me about a doctor that he found to be impressive. He had helped him to stop smoking with one healing session. I decided to visit this man in nearby Schwäbisch Hall. His name was Dr. Fritsche, and he was an iridologist. This is someone who examines the pupils of your eyes and then gives a diagnosis. I had never heard of this before. During this initial appointment, I was somewhat startled as I observed his eyes moving back and forth in a strange motion, as if he was thoroughly scanning me with his eyes. I had never seen anything like this before.

He analyzed my pupils for a while and then put an enlarged picture of them up on a big screen. He described my symptoms precisely and said that my immune system had been stripped with all of the antibiotics. He also described many other things about me perfectly, including my deepest beliefs and significant occurrences in my life. Then he started to tell me many things that happened to me in my childhood. He told me that I was brutally raped as a child and repeatedly beaten and now someone close to me was betraying me and that this was what was now causing my illness. He said that my body was trying to get my attention in the only way it knew how, namely with a fever and sickness. I thought that he must have been mistaken or that he had me confused with someone else. I thought, *I would remember that!* I completely dismissed everything he said and did not even take it seriously for one second. He prescribed some probiotics to strengthen my immune system and recommended that I make an appointment with his colleague who was also an alternative health practitioner.

I did go to see this woman. It was my first time to see someone who practiced kinesiology. Although I didn't really understand all that she was doing in testing how my muscles responded to the various statements she made, it appeared she knew her profession well and was confident and experienced. The belief in kinesiology is that all of the information from the subconscious mind is stored in the body and can be recovered when we test the muscles. She went through the various levels of the physical, mental, spiritual, and emotional body. When she advanced to the spiritual and emotional levels, many things started to surface. When she found that I had been hurt by a religious authority figure, she became very upset. She asked me, "Which religious authority figure hurt you?"

I could not think of anything. I said, "One time a nun pinched my earlobe."

Her voice got louder, and she became more upset and said, "No! That isn't it. It is much more traumatic! Think! *Think!*" I thought of one time when my piano teacher hit my fingers with a ruler. She said, "No, that's not it!" Nothing else came to my mind. She said she could not help me on these deep emotional levels where this trauma was stored. She told me to call her if I would like to see her again or if I remembered what this was. I didn't believe her or take this too seriously, as I really thought I would remember if I had experienced something as traumatic as what she made it sound like. I was a little bothered because she was so upset.

That night Michael called and asked me if I would like to go out for a nice dinner together to our favorite place, which we only went to on our anniversary or other special occasions. He said that he had something important to ask me. I thought, *Oh, finally we are going to build the house we have always dreamed about, and he is ready to settle down and have a normal life.* Instead he broke the news that the president of the company asked him to move to China for one year. There were problems with the subsidiary there, and it was believed that someone in authority was stealing millions of dollars.

By this time Michael had fired so many people and reorganized so many companies all over Europe and Asia that they had nicknamed him "the Terminator." He had often spoken about being at war with the managing director in China. I felt as though this hardness of heart that he brought to his job was spilling over into our family life and home.

I did not in any way want to move to China. Marie had just gotten settled back into school in Germany and was having a rough time, already being the different kid. She had missed about one fourth of all school days because of fever and bronchitis. And now she was suffering because of it. I could not see any positive reason why we should move again and back into a highly polluted country.

I did not want to search for new friends in a new culture again while he traveled around the world, leaving us alone in a foreign country. In Germany we had our friends and his family, and we were surrounded by beautiful nature. We had a really nice life for the most part despite my illness. We could also breathe freely in Germany. After we lived in Asia for so long, we were thrilled to have plenty of fresh air again. Every time we landed in America or Germany while we were living in Asia, we would stop the car after we left the airport and get out and just breathe in the fresh air.

In addition, Shanghai was a seventeen-hour flight to Minneapolis compared to Frankfurt, which was around eleven hours. So living in Asia made it more difficult for me to visit my family. The last time we moved to Asia for what should have been one year, we returned almost eight years later. Furthermore, I had packed and unpacked so many cardboard boxes in the previous years after eight consecutive moves that I was packing and unpacking boxes in my dreams for weeks after the last move.

He continued to try to convince me to move. He told me how this move would further his career and that we could save enough money to build the house we had been dreaming about. He is a born salesman and is extremely persuasive. He even invited good friends of ours from the company to tell me all about Shanghai, as they had lived there for a year and had loved it! They showed me many great photographs of their year in Shanghai. They also pointed out several pieces of beautiful and very inexpensive furniture in their home that they had bought there. Michael said it would be my job to find us nice furniture and artwork for our new house we could build as soon as we returned. He insisted enough that I eventually agreed. I felt bulldozed into moving while in a weakened state. We made arrangements to move a few months later during the school break in August.

I went back to see the alternative health practitioner, and I told her we were moving to China. She said, "What? You cannot go to China until you figure out what is wrong with you! This is serious!" I told her that I felt I had no choice. She said, "Oh dear, may I try tapping (emotional freedom technique also known as EFT) on you?" It was a new technique that she had just learned at a seminar. I was willing to try it if she avoided tapping where my head was still tender. As she tapped on my energy meridian points, she tried to teach me at the same time how to do this to heal myself. She sent me home with a wall chart and instructions. I tried it a few times but did not understand its significance. At that time I did not realize how effective it could be in releasing pain, trauma, and stress.

Every part of my being did not want to move to Shanghai. I had a very sickening feeling about it. I felt so weak that it was difficult to pack or do all of the necessary cleaning that was required when one is moving. I was resisting so strongly that I could not find our passports shortly before we were supposed to be picked up for the airport. I did find them at the last minute packed inside my suitcase. It was as though my feet were dragging while I was forcing myself out the front door. I had flown and moved so many times since I had married Michael; however, I had never felt so much intense evil, and my mind was never as scattered as those weeks before that move. Everything felt wrong!

Help Was on the Way

We moved to Shanghai in August of 2004. Michael went there three weeks before us and found a two-story apartment in a high-rise building in a gated community called Season's Villas. It was in the newly built section of Shanghai called Pudong. Within the walls of these gates, it was like a separate little Western city. Thankfully the staff spoke English. There was a community center, playground, restaurant, grocery store, post office, fitness center, and most importantly, a very nice international school right across the street from our building. There was also a small bus that took us to church in the city on the opposite side of the river Huangpu, which was called Pu Xi. We needed our passports to attend the Catholic and other Christian churches, but they existed for the expats. I was very grateful that we did not have to live in the chaos that existed outside of these walls.

When we arrived in Shanghai, I almost felt as if I had landed on another planet. Many things seemed to be completely upside down from how I thought that they should be. And in regards to energy, it felt like the complete opposite of the tranquility of Japan. Everything felt false and wrong.

This city was not like anything I had ever seen before. The contrast between the wealth of the elite few and the poverty of the majority was immediately apparent. The Huangpu River divides Shanghai into two distinct districts—the new modern section, which is called Pudong, and the original city, which is called Pu Xi.

The Pudong district displays a wide range of skyscrapers, many of which are the largest in the world. There are many architecturally distinctive and even eccentric buildings throughout the city. To me, it appeared as though they had copied many famous buildings from several cities in the world and increased the size just to say that they had the largest in the world.

On the Pu Xi side of the river, there are many impressive examples of contemporary architecture, beautiful pieces of Soviet architecture, and a large number of art deco buildings all mixed together with the traditional Chinese dwellings called Shikumen. These are simple and small, one- or two-story, old and impoverished homes. Many are open to the elements. People can easily see inside of them while they are driving by. My opinion is that the city is a strange but interesting blend of the wealthy modern and the poverty-stricken traditional. I had never seen anything like it before.

The pollution was thick and dark gray most of the time. When outside, I found it difficult to breathe with the mixture of extreme summer heat and smog. We could not even open a window, as the stinky polluted air would bellow in. We usually did not see the sun or sky for weeks at a time. Occasionally there was a typhoon, and the strong winds would blow away the pollution enough so that it was comfortable and one could see the sky.

Although I had shoveled plenty of manure growing up on the farm, the mix of smells combined with the heat made the pig barn from the farm smell almost pleasant in comparison. In Shanghai, there are many traditional one-room homes that have no plumbing, and it was known that all of the waste was dumped into the river that flowed through the city. On a hot day there was no mistake as to what one could smell.

Within a week of moving into our apartment, the same friend who had previously lived in Shanghai came to visit us. Her name is Julianne, and she is one of the nicest, most down-to-earth and positive people I know. I admire how extremely outgoing and adventurous she is. There were still some places in China that she wanted to see, including the yellow mountains.

She offered to show me where the best hospitals, doctors, and dentists were, and she pointed out where the German butchers and bakeries were. I was kind of surprised that there were German butchers and bakers in Shanghai, and I could find some authentic sausages, pretzels, and rolls, which were a staple in my husband's diet. I had the feeling that there was nothing one could not purchase in this massive city if you had the money. This was sickeningly clear in the four- or five-star hotels that catered to the Western businessmen. I felt as though I had stepped into a shady world that I did not know previously existed and I wished I could immediately step out of it again.

During my tour of the city with our friend showing me the most essential things for our stay in Shanghai, there were three different times that three different people handed me the exact same thin magazine with advertising in it as I entered their shop, hotel, or business. Every time this magazine was opened to exactly the same page. Amazingly, the second and third time it was handed to me one small advertisement was standing out of the page and flashing in big bold letters about four inches larger. It read, "If you are looking for clarity and peace of mind, please call Karen at 0186#######." This felt like a wake up call. I did not call Karen right away, but I definitely felt that I should. I kept the number.

Shortly after that, I became very sick with pneumonia. The doctor told me that if I did not get better within twenty-four hours, he would need to admit me to the hospital. I worried about who would take care of Marie. I hoped that my husband would, but as driven and as focused as he was on his work, I doubted that he would take time off to take care of her, as he had not taken one hour to watch her since her birth. He seemed to be far away from us, and we rarely saw him. He was very busy firing many people and reorganizing a very large company. I did not want her to be alone in a foreign country with a stranger, and I did not want to be in a hospital in China. I did not yet know anyone except her teachers. Once again I got down on my knees like never before. When I recovered, I had a new determination to get to the root of this illness once and for all.

I went one last time to a doctor in hopes of finding out what the fever was caused by. He could not find anything and told me that I was just a spoiled white woman who was looking for attention. I knew that this was not true, and so this angered me and fired up my determination. Following this, I finally listened to my intuition, which was telling me to call Karen.

She was very kind on the phone. She was from Hong Kong, and her English was excellent. I made an appointment to visit her at her apartment. The taxi driver dropped me off about a thirty-minute walk from her high-rise complex. Because I had lived overseas for so long, I knew to always carry with me the address of my home and my desired destination written in English and the native language. We hadn't been in China for long, so I did not know that taxi drivers in Shanghai might drop you off quite a distance from your desired address if it was more convenient for them. I later discovered that this was common knowledge among the expats.

I managed to easily find her. I am not exactly sure how, as the city blocks were very long and there were few signs in English. I felt as though my footsteps were being guided. I had seen large apartment buildings in Asia before, especially in Jakarta, Indonesia, and Kuala Lumpur, the capital city of Malaysia, but this was the most massive concrete apartment complex I had ever seen. To me, some of the apartment complexes in China resembled something from a sci-fi movie.

She offered me some warm tea and asked me to be seated. After she talked with me a while, she said very politely, "I cannot help you because your problems are spiritual. But I know someone who can. Her name is Mabel. She is a spiritual healer and hypnotherapist. I know she can help you."

I thought, *Oh boy, hypnotherapy? I don't really want to have hypnotherapy. But I do want to get to the bottom of this, and I want my life back!* I decided to call her.

She put me on the phone with Mabel so I could speak with her. I immediately felt comforted, as she sounded like a kind, caring, and wise grandmother. Her voice sounded familiar, like that of an old friend, and yet that wasn't possible. She was also from Hong Kong, and her English was very good. After we talked for a while, I agreed to meet her the next day at her home.

The Spiritual Healer

I was hesitant and somewhat afraid, but I knew I needed to see her. I arranged for my husband's driver to take me. As I did not speak Chinese and he did not speak English, I asked my husband's secretary to ask him to come in and get me if I did not come out within a certain time frame.

We traveled for more than an hour across to the other side of the city. When I met Mabel for the first time, I was surprised because she was not an elderly grandmother at all but a beautiful and very young-looking woman who was only three years older than I. Her house was cozy and decorated with many pictures, pillows, and artwork with angels. She asked me to sit on her couch and handed me a mug of water with Archangel Michael on it. I wondered, *How could she know?* On the couch was a pillow with an embroidered picture of Archangel Michael to my right, and to my left there was one with Archangel Raphael. As I had prayed to St. Michael since I was a little girl, I felt immediately comfortable, even though the entire situation seemed surreal. Although I felt that this was not a coincidence, I did not know Mabel well enough to distinguish if she was genuine or not, so I still had my guard up.

We talked for around one and a half hours. She told me about her background. Her real name is NG, Mae Bo, in Chinese. Traditionally Chinese use their surnames first. Many of them have a Western name they use for their Western friends or business contacts. Obviously she chose Mabel because it most resembles Mae Bo. She was born into a Buddhist family and attended a Christian school for six years and Catholic school for one year. Later she went on a journey of self-discovery and went to India and studied Tibetan Buddhism with traditional monks under the Dalai Lama. Following that, she moved to China and studied Taoism.

She asked me several questions. Some of them were about the illness, pain, and the fear or presence of something evil that I was experiencing. She asked me what my biggest fears were as well as my spiritual beliefs and if I believed in God, Jesus, and angels. As I was sitting there on her couch, I told her that I felt like I was broken into a million pieces but did not know why. I remember that there was so much pressure in my head that my eyes were heavy and it was difficult to keep them open. I just wanted to sleep.

As we were conversing, I saw with my peripheral vision someone standing to my right. I shared with her that I could often see what looked like a man out of the corner of my right eye on my right side. Whenever I turned, there was no one there. It didn't scare me, but I felt it was of some significance. She told me that this represented a male relative on my father's side. She asked me to close my eyes and ask the person what his name was. I did as she asked, and in complete disbelief I heard a name, not out loud but with my inner voice, my intuition. I heard the name John. This was my dad's and my younger brother's name. It is a very common name, so I didn't really think much about it at the time.

I told her that my biggest fear was that one of Marie's teachers would hurt her at school. I also had the fear that someone would break into our apartment and rape me. I did not have this fear when I was younger but only in recent years. Although I didn't understand these fears, I thought that they were just common fears. I also told her that I often woke up in a panic in the previous years, feeling like I was suffocating and someone was choking me. I knew that if I had faith, I was not supposed to live in fear, and I wished that I did not have these fears.

She asked me if we could speak to my pain. She taught me from this first meeting on to speak to the pain and ask it if it had a name. She then asked what message it had for me, or what it wanted to teach me. This was very strange for me, as I had never heard of this before. However, when I tried it together with her, I was astonished to hear a name and a message.

She continued in further appointments to teach me to send the pain love and light. Usually the pain disappeared. At this time, I had really bad pain in my knees from falling so often and occasionally it was as though my legs were paralyzed.

She told me that she heard the angels say that I would benefit from hypnotherapy, regression, and past-life regression. I was quite skeptical when she told me she could hear what the angels were saying. I wondered, *Is this really possible?* Up until this time in my life I had never met anyone who could hear what God and the angels were saying. Honestly I thought at the time that what she said was kind of cheesy. I had lived the previous thirteen years in a foreign country, was fairly isolated as every time Marie and I made friends we moved, had no television in English except CNN and BBC, and had a limited supply to books in English. I think if I had been living in the United States, I possibly would have been exposed to more healers or individuals who had this ability.

As a Catholic, I was hesitant to try past-life regression because I believed we only have one life, this life, and that it was wrong to even contemplate the idea of more lives. However, because I had the inexplicable distinct feeling that I knew and greatly loved my husband immediately upon looking into his eyes for the very first time, I believed that past lives might be possible. She asked me if we could close our eyes together and say a prayer asking to be guided about whether or not I should try hypnotherapy and past-life regression. I agreed, but I did not think that she could persuade me, as I am fairly stubborn in my beliefs. She did not have to, as someone else did and he was wholly undeniable.

Meeting Archangel Raphael—"He who Heals"

I agreed to pray with her. She lit a white candle and made the intention of welcoming only the highest vibrating beings from heaven. She asked that we be protected with the white light of God. She then said one of the most beautiful prayers I had ever heard, thanking God, our heavenly Father, Jesus, the Holy Spirit, the archangels Raphael, Michael, Gabriel, and Uriel, and our guardian angels that they were present with us. She told me that we invoked Archangel Raphael for healing, Michael for protection,

Gabriel for communication, and Uriel for wisdom and forgiveness. She explained to me that they are always immediately present when we asked and that they could be in all places at all times. She asked for the angels to make it known to me if I should proceed with hypnotherapy, regression, and past-life regression. She asked me to close my eyes and listen with my heart.

Almost immediately I heard an increasingly loud "Yes, yes, *yes!*" All of a sudden I opened my eyes and saw a big strong angel standing right in front of me. I knew instantly that it was Archangel Raphael. He looked like he was ten feet tall. I first saw a white robe that went slightly below his knees. His calves were strong and very big in diameter. He was wearing some very interesting brown sandals that went halfway up his calves. They reminded me of the ones the Roman gladiators are depicted as wearing in paintings and movies. I could not see his face, as it was covered with a white mist that was emanating a great amount of bright white light.

Wow! I was completely astonished. I had not in any way expected this. He was huge and powerful and yet very loving and gentle. I felt like he was saying, "Everything will be all right." I instantly knew that he knew me inside and out from the very beginning of time and that he loved me very much. I also loved him instantly like we were old friends or as if he were my big brother. I knew he was there to help me. I felt great comfort, and I was certain that I would finally be healed. I made an appointment to come back the next day for my first hypnotherapy session. I did not need to think twice or rationalize any longer about whether or not this was the right thing to do. He convinced me without even saying a word!

Stepping into the Spiritual Realms

From this moment on it seemed my entire world was split open. I was living in the physical world but could now see into the spirit world. My life became saturated with angelic visitations, trips to heaven, and other highly spiritual experiences throughout the next years. My dreams, prayer time, meditation, hypnotherapy, and also normal waking hours were filled with angels in many different forms. Throughout the first years I saw them just as in the beautiful renaissance paintings where they are depicted as wearing elegant flowing gowns. I also saw them as bright white luminescent beings, and as sparkling or glowing lights of various sizes and colors. Later I often saw angels and archangels as moving energy that was bright white, golden, purple, blue, green, orange, pink, yellow, or copper-colored. There is, however, no painting, regardless of how marvelous it is, that can capture the beauty or the love emanating from any of the heavenly beings I encountered.

I consider these angelic visitations and journeys to heaven to be the most awe-inspiring thing that any human could possibly experience while still on the earth. I felt truly honored and blessed. I understood that this was a gift and a privilege. However, to suddenly have my spiritual vision opened to everything in the spirit realms, including demons in many forms, people in heaven, and countless people who had died but had not yet gone to heaven, was for me extremely traumatic. For several years I felt that this was a curse and not a blessing. I just wanted to be normal. Besides the trauma of experiencing so many inconceivable and frightening events, it was especially difficult feeling like I was the only one and could tell no one as who could possibly understand this. I honestly do not think I could have withstood being exposed to the dark entities and these other realms without constant help and comfort from the angels, who never left my side. I did have Mabel to help me throughout the first year and we continued to correspond for several years after this.

My intention in briefly writing about the darkness I encountered is not to instill fear or to shock anyone. I believe that each of us lives with or has encountered some level of fear or darkness or know someone close to us who has. I feel that the power of the fear is removed when it is demystified, and then healing may occur. My hope is that you are inspired to see that I am just a normal woman who survived this battle by asking heaven to intervene for me. And heaven responded in remarkable ways.

I would like to clarify some things. As I had mentioned earlier, I have always loved angels, and I believed that they existed; however, I was not sure if they really existed in our day and age. I remember praying to the angels for protection since I was a little girl, not even knowing exactly why, except that I felt comforted. The first small present I ever remember receiving from my mom was a set of two one-inch-tall ceramic angels, and I still have them today. I have many angel statues in my home of all different materials and sizes. Most of these were given to me as gifts over the years for singing or helping someone. I have sung in public since I was around ten or twelve years old. It began at church and school musicals. Then I was asked to sing at weddings and wedding showers. So, already as a teenager, my bedroom shelves were full of knickknacks in the form of angels.

In addition, my husband often called me an earth angel, and so had my best friend and roommate in college. I was also used to people telling me that I was "too good for this earth." I knew what they meant, as that was how I felt about some of my siblings. I even had that very real angelic encounter at the time of the fire and the vision of the giant illuminated praying hands.

However, I was not in any way prepared for what was about to happen in my life. Because of the intense evil I was encountering at the same time,

I felt like I had been pushed into a cold, deep ocean in the middle of a dark, violent storm, and I knew I had to keep swimming and clinging to Jesus and the angels instructions in order to survive. In the very worst of times during the most recent years, it was also the love I had for my daughter that pulled me through and gave me the strength and determination to survive when I felt as though the one closest to me was crushing my spirit.

Regarding these heavenly experiences, I had never imagined this or wished for this or even thought that this was possible. In fact, just a few years before I met Mabel, I was invited to my Australian neighbor's house in Singapore for a healing workshop. Although I liked her, I was not interested in going. But because I had declined her invitations so often, I felt obligated. She practiced several types of alternative healing. That particular evening was a class on developing the intuition. Her distinguished friend from Australia was the guest speaker and she was excellent. Everyone there was very welcoming and kind, but I felt uncomfortable after I overheard the two women seated next to me discussing how they hoped to meet their guardian angels that night. Honestly I thought, *Oh, my gosh, get me out of here and away from all of these weirdoes!* Now years later I am one of those same weirdoes.

So before this time I was still fairly skeptical and not purposely seeking angelic encounters, soul travel, or out-of-body experiences as I know some people are hoping for today. All of this was the furthest from my mind. My only thought was one of survival for my husband, daughter, and family.

I would also like to take this opportunity to say that what I have written is my 100 percent authentic account of what I experienced. I do not want to debate anyone, but I would be willing to take any lie-detector test that what I have written here is my honest chronicle of what I underwent. I wrote the portion of the book about my experiences in heaven and with the angels all within two days, as it was only a matter of writing it down. It is entirely divinely inspired and I have known for several years that I needed to write it. Initially I was not going to write more about myself, but then felt I was called to add my life journey until this time and what led me to the point of seeking help from a spiritual healer. Believe me that this narration goes so far beyond anything I could possibly even begin to imagine. If anything, I dulled it down so it would not sound quite as outrageous and unbelievable.

I know that there are things that I have forgotten, as the knowledge shared with me was often so vast and beyond my comprehension or limited understanding that I could not grasp it all. But the things I have written here were shown to me many times, and I am certain of them.

I have not included in this book what my personal opinion is or swayed the information according to the doctrine that I follow, but I adhered strictly to what I learned in heaven from God and the angels.

I have grouped many of my most memorable experiences in heaven into one section in the book, as I felt it would be easier to follow. Otherwise my experiences are in chronological order as they occurred. Every single encounter was different, and I was taken many times back and forth between heaven and earth, a realm in between heaven and earth, past lives (past-life regression), and childhood (regression). I was also taken twice to a time when I was seated together with God in heaven before I returned to earth. These meetings with God and a visitation from the holy family were possibly my most incredible experiences of all. It was then that I received the greatest revelation and the most important lessons and messages. Every session was accompanied and directed by angels.

Healing Sessions with Mabel

The angels guided every session I ever had with Mabel. She made it very clear to me that she was only a vessel that God worked through. She helped me reach a state of deep relaxation, guided me to open my spiritual vision, rigorously took notes, and encouraged forgiveness when needed. However, everything else was entirely up to the angels, and they chose the exact order that things would be revealed to me for healing and instruction. The angels decided whether I would have lessons in heaven, regress back to my childhood, or revisit past lives.

I had undeniable verification after every session that what I had experienced was real. The signs came in many forms, and they were beyond coincidence and what could be accidental signals, clues, and symbols.

What Mabel did during the first session and continued to do was teach me how to tune in to my own intuition. She told me that everyone has the ability to hear God's voice if they take the time to be still, quiet their minds, and listen. Everyone can access answers to the questions they have through prayer and meditation. We all have access at any minute of the day to the wisdom and knowledge of our souls and highest selves, which retain all of the knowledge learned throughout every lifetime ever lived.

She also told me that the angels said that they would be working with me in my dreams. Therefore, I should write down what I could remember from my dreams and discuss them with her when I saw her. The dreams I had at that time were absolutely incredible and unlike any dreams I had ever had before. I often wished I could somehow capture them or keep them to watch over and over again, as they were saturated with splendorous beauty, love, knowledge, healing, and powerful messages.

I always felt very comfortable, as Mabel never once said that I should come back for more sessions. She also did not at any point encourage me to become dependent on her. Instead she taught me during my very first appointment with her and every subsequent visit how to connect with heaven and to listen to my own intuition to heal myself. She also asked me to remain in a state of receiving. The main thing she was very insistent on was that I develop a consistent spiritual practice. She encouraged me to keep praying and meditate twice a day for at least ten minutes.

I would like to add that hypnotherapy helped me tremendously because my childhood wounds were buried deep in my subconscious, and I honestly do not know how else I would have ever retrieved them. For me it was like being given a life-saving key that opened locked-up memories. I had to experience them again in order to believe that these things really occurred. I did not believe that it was possible for me to have experienced something that I could not remember. It was essential in my healing from the unexplained illness, fever, and evil presence I was experiencing. However, I would only recommend this if it is truly necessary and not for entertainment purposes. This should only be done with a licensed hypnotherapist and someone who understands the importance of spiritual protection before entering these realms. I believe hypnotherapy and past-life regression can open doors to these other realms, and one needs to be prepared for and be under the care of someone who knows how to navigate another safely through these realms.

CHAPTER

The Healing Begins

T he following morning after my first appointment with Mabel, I woke up and again saw Archangel Raphael. This time he was standing directly in front of me at the foot of my bed. My eyes were open. I knew instantly that it was him. He emanated strength and love and was around ten feet tall. He was holding a five- or six-foot-long scepter with a clear ball on the end of it. The ball was about the size of a bowling ball and was radiating a great amount of brilliant emerald green light. He first held the end of the scepter with the ball over my head. Then he held this ball over my heart for a longer time. Every time I close my eyes to pray or meditate or say his name to this day, I still see this beautiful green light. My feeling is that he has stayed with me from that day on.

I was completely astonished and startled, and I felt renewed enthusiasm and strength. I also felt an incredible sense of significance that I had not felt before because this magnificent being from heaven visited me, again! Following this, my entire life as I knew it was changed forever.

I arrived for my appointment with Mabel at 9:00 a.m., and I told her about my second visitation from Archangel Raphael. She appeared happy to hear about it, but she didn't seem overly surprised. She said that she had been working with the angelic realm for more than seven years and that they always came when we asked.

Mabel shared with me that she had already been preparing for my session for several hours. I had never met anyone so dedicated to his or her spiritual practice before. She got up every day at 5:00 a.m. and spent several hours in prayer and meditation. She practiced Kundalini yoga. She followed a strict vegetarian diet and also spent many weeks during the year fasting. She traveled several times a year to India, where she helped sponsor some homes for orphaned children and continued to study with her Tibetan monk friends. She was constantly teaching others and learning new healing skills. After many months in her company, I learned that she most aspired to be like Jesus.

Before we began my first hypnotherapy session, she lit a white candle and invited the angels to be with us. We prayed together, and she began by surrounding us both with the white light of God for protection. She invited only the highest vibrating celestial beings to be with us. The prayers she spoke were simple and beautiful. I wished later that I had recorded them. Every time she thanked God, Jesus, the Holy Spirit, and the archangels Michael, Raphael, Gabriel, and Uriel for being with us. She again told me that we summoned Archangel Michael for Protection, Archangel Raphael for healing, Archangel Gabriel for communication, and Archangel Uriel for wisdom and forgiveness. She offered prayers of praise, thanksgiving, petition, and agreement that I be healed.

Hypnotherapy was not what I had expected. Mabel guided me into a deep state of relaxation. I found that I was quickly and easily able to relax deeply, possibly from the several years of listening to self-hypnosis cassettes when I was younger and the transcendental meditation I had practiced while I was living in Singapore. Although I was in a deep state of relaxation, I was more acutely aware of my senses and everything around me than I had ever been in a normal state of being fully awake. She asked me to look around in this realm of my subconscious mind and see if I recognized anyone. What happened next was astounding, and I remember it very clearly to this day.

All of a sudden I was in a big beautiful room that looked like it belonged to royalty. It reminded me of one of the reception rooms that I had often seen while I was touring the castles in Bavaria. It was decorated with white molding that splendidly trimmed the high ceiling. The walls were soft pink, blue, and yellow and I immediately felt at home. First I saw cherub-looking angels twirling around near the ceiling. I knew that they were welcoming me and I felt immediate joy. Although they looked like chubby human babies, I knew that they were wise. Their elbows were interlocked. The scene resembled the square dancing we had occasionally rehearsed in grade school, except they were twirling around in midair. There were a few small pretty clouds and what looked like a yellow star in the center of the room. Then I realized that the entire room was completely full of angels. There were several large guardian angels and other angels of all sizes. They were wearing flowing gowns of mostly pastel colors, gold, and white. I felt their love for me. I knew that they were all happy to see me, and they welcomed me. I was in complete awe. It was as if we knew one another, and I felt extremely safe, which was very important because of what was about to occur.

What happened next was horrifying. I am not sure if I could have endured it without the comforting presence of the angels. A horrible, loud, deep, dark, male voice started fiercely shouting at Mabel. Shockingly this voice was coming out of my mouth! I recognized this voice as a similar voice to what I had heard when I was in that church service in Singapore when the woman was being exorcised. He was shouting every possible profanity at Mabel. I had never heard some of the words he used before. It was as if they were from an ancient foreign language. I have an abnormally high speaking voice, so much so that when people I do not know call our home and I answer the phone, they sometimes ask, "Is your mother home?" This voice was booming and angry and fierce. He told her to leave me alone. He said that I was none of her business and she should go away and leave me be. Suddenly I could see him. He was huge and looked like a hideous beast that was similar to a gargoyle or one of those ugly creatures from *The Lord of the Rings.*

I am someone who could not even watch many scenes in the trilogy of those movies, and I needed to fast-forward through any scenes with orcs and all the battle scenes. I avoided horror movies and everything dark my entire life. Now I was living my worst fear. I wondered, *How can this possibly be? Is this really happening to me?*

Mabel began to speak with this being in the most loving but authoritative voice. She was skillful, calm, and well experienced, I could tell. He resisted and continued to yell back at her. She asked him what his name was. He answered with the name Magnus.

Mabel continued to speak in the most loving but firm voice. She told him about God. She asked him why he was by me. He replied that it was his job to stop me from my mission. He said if he did not succeed, he would be continually tortured forever. He said there were many more like him by me, but he was the leader and the biggest and strongest.

She told him that he had a Father in heaven who loved him very much and that all he had to do was say, "Father, forgive me," and he could return to a loving home in heaven. There he would be safe, and he could not be tortured anymore. She explained to him that this apology must be sincere. She told him that what he was seeking was this original love of God, his Father in heaven. She explained to him more about this love and his true home. Magnus did not believe her. He said it sounded too good to be true.

Then she did many things to muster and amplify this light and this love of God and sent it directly to the beast's mind and heart. She used the bright white light of God. She also used the more golden yellow light of Jesus, which shown bright as the sun. The entire room was filled with light, and a strong wind began to blow as the presence of the Holy Spirit entered the room. Mabel was waving her arms up and down in big sweeping motions to help this beast feel the presence and the love of God and encourage it to go to the light. This seemed to go on for a while, and she did many other things, including invoking St. Michael and his army of angels. He came immediately. This was the first time I ever saw St. Michael. He was absolutely astonishing. He was more handsome than any man I have ever seen, and he was also strong, loving, confident, and powerful. He was dressed as a warrior in golden armor and was holding a sword with a great amount of white light shining from it. He arrived with many strong warrior angels. I am not sure how many there were in his army, but I believe at least fifty. From my experience the number of warrior angels that exist is unlimited. I wish I could in some way recreate this for anyone reading this book or show you what I still see in my mind from that day. I believe it would be more incredible than any man-made movie could ever portray or recreate.

She touched and tapped on the beast's forehead with her right middle finger as if she wanted to wake him up. All of a sudden the beast felt this love of God and truly seemed to wake up. It was as though he then knew the truth and accepted it. Mabel asked God if he could come to heaven. God said, "Yes." Mabel instructed the beast to say, "Father, forgive me." The beast repeated after her and said, "Father, forgive me."

Then she asked the beast to apologize to me for the ways he had hurt me. He apologized. She asked me if I would forgive him, and I did. I did not want in any way to delay or inhibit this process.

Immediately he began to rise in the air and was transmuted before our very eyes into his original form, which was a human man. He was spinning slowly around in bright sparking golden and white light as he was being transformed. I had seen the movie *Beauty and the Beast* several years before this when Marie was young. When I saw the movie again a while after this experience, it reminded me very much of the scene at the end of the movie when the beast changes back into a man, except this beast was far more grotesque-looking than the one in the movie. After this, we saw angels escorting him to heaven. After he was in heaven, he thanked Mabel many times. He was now aware of his true self on a soul level and was at complete peace. He told us that there were many more beings like him by me that needed to come to heaven and the light. He then encouraged the other demons to come to heaven, and he told them how loving and safe it was.

With this, Mabel asked God if they could come to heaven too. God said, "Yes." Mabel coached them on asking God for forgiveness. They all said, "God, forgive me" or "Father, forgive me." Again she asked them to apologize to me, and they did. She asked me if I would forgive them, and I agreed.

Immediately they started emerging from my body and began rising one by one toward the angels and the light of heaven. I could feel them in various ways coming up my throat and out of my mouth. I don't know exactly how many there were, but there were many, as it was an army of demons. They were in all different shapes and sizes. There were many that resembled gargoyles, sea creatures, or reptiles and others that resembled giant insects. None of them looked like the beautiful mammals we see on the earth. In addition, none of the sea creatures resembled the stunning colorful fish found near the coral reef, but rather ugly octopi, squid, and the strange looking creatures found at the bottom of the ocean. Some of them resembled black Pac-Man figures, black balls with eyes and several sharp teeth. Most of them were horrendously ugly. I could feel that all of them were ashamed of how they looked, and this shame was part of the manipulation. They said that they were part of an army and their assignment was to keep me from my mission. I was shocked! I thought, *Who? Me?* And yet deep down it all made sense to me, though I did not completely understand why.

As each of them rose toward heaven, they were greeted and escorted by an angel into paradise. Before they reached heaven, they were each transformed back into their original forms, human men. At this time I saw several angels thoroughly cleaning all the areas inside my body where these beings had been. They were using bright white brooms and cloths

Mabel then spoke with them in heaven after they were safe and at peace. They were extremely grateful to now be free and home again. I was shown by the angels how these souls, God's original creation, had been stolen by Satan from this lower realm between heaven and earth and made to do the work of Satan on the earth. The angels told me how the love and light of God are the most powerful tools and weapons in the universe and that there is no amount of darkness that is as powerful as the love of God.

I was then aware that God was with us, and I was allowed to feel the overwhelming and unconditional fatherly love that he felt for these souls and how grateful he was to have them returned home to him again.

I would prefer not to write about darkness and demons in this book, as I want to focus on the light and love of God and on heaven. But at the same time I feel it is one of the most important messages that God wants me to bring to the world. We must be certain of our belonging to God, and we must be aware of his tremendous love and mercy for all of us and not allow our hearts to become hardened so that our souls are not vulnerable to Satan.

I understand that many people do not want to believe that Satan is real and that they prefer to call it negative energy or ego. I believe that all of these things exist in various forms and degrees and can also work as resistance against us, but what I saw many times was a real being that looked very similar to how he is depicted in renaissance art—an ugly, tall, skinny red and black being with long, pointy ears.

What was particularly impressed upon my heart was the fact that God is the only Creator. Every single soul is created in his light and in his image. These dark entities were formerly what God called *lost souls* and were stuck in a realm between heaven and earth. While in this realm they were captured by Satan to do his work on the earth. Most importantly, God's love and mercy are so great that he wants all of these lost souls, if they sincerely repent and accept him as their Father, to return to the light and to heaven. In my observance it was consistent that the acceptance or acknowledgement of him as their Father and Savior superseded the repentance.

Over the course of the next year I was repeatedly shown this realm between heaven and earth, the cycle of life and death, and exactly how these souls got to this horrific state where they were transmuted through the usage of their own guilt, fear, and shame into these ugly creatures. We typically call these beings *demons* or *dark entities*. They were then tortured by Satan to do his work on the earth. This is what God wants to stop. He does not want to lose even one of his children. I have written more about this in the chapter called "The Lost Souls," as I feel that bringing forth this truth is one of my main assignments in writing this book.

That was the end of my first hypnotherapy session. It took me at least thirty minutes before I could move or open my eyes. When I emerged from this deep state of consciousness and heightened awareness, I realized that what had seemed like a thirty-minute session had actually been two and a half hours long.

Everything I had just experienced was shocking. To see and experience real demons was like my worst fear being realized. Now I knew that they existed. I thought that they did because the Bible mentions them numerous times. I had definitely felt them and seen them since moving to Singapore. What encouraged me was seeing how easily Mabel, who used the light and love of God, together with St. Michael and his army of angels defeated them, or brought them back to the light. I was especially grateful and overwhelmed that this magnificent and powerful archangel came immediately to help *me* despite my feeling so weak, insignificant, and unimportant. Of course, it also helped to see that Mabel had complete control of this unbelievably frightening situation, and it was clear to me that God was working with her and through her. She told me several times that she was just a normal woman who allowed God to work through her.

Much of what I had just witnessed presented me with entirely new concepts. It was difficult for me to believe that God would welcome a demon back into heaven and that he was this merciful and inclusive. In addition, that all of these demons were formerly normal human beings with souls created by God just like me. I feel I was given great empathy for these souls on that day. Most importantly I understood that God is not limited regarding his love and mercy. It was only I who was limited in my beliefs of how I thought God's love and mercy should be.

Everything I had just witnessed caused me to question almost my entire belief system. I knew that what I had just experienced was real. There was not one doubt in my mind.

Mabel commended me on my ability to forgive these demons that had disrupted my life for so long and caused me so much spiritual torment and pain. At the time I was thinking that it was much easier to forgive them and allow them to leave me and ascend to heaven than to hold onto them and keep them with me. For me there was no doubt in my mind or choice as to whether I should forgive them or not as I felt God was asking me too. It was incredible to me that after they returned to heaven we could still see them now as men and they were thanking us for our help. They even promised to help us back in return in whatever way they could from heaven.

She told me that it was imperative to bring these former demons to the light because otherwise they would latch onto someone else if we only removed them.

Mabel repeated what the angels had said about how the love and light of God are the most powerful tools and weapons in the entire universe. She said that there is no amount of negative energy that is as powerful as the love of God.

She then explained to me more about all of the light I had just witnessed. She revealed to me that the light of God is pure bright white and the light of Jesus is more yellowish like the sun. She told me that if I bring even the smallest light or candle into the darkest room, the room is no longer dark. This statement was very powerful to me and I never forgot it.

She said that the angels told her that I needed to learn to use the love and light of God to do what she had done, specifically transmute dark or negative energy back to light by using the love and light of God. I thought, *Who? Me? No way! I could never do that!* I told her that I didn't think I could ever do what she had just done. She said very firmly, "Yes, you have to learn. I will teach you!" This blew my mind. How did they possibly expect me to do this? A few days before I was so weak that I was having a hard time just keeping my eyes open and my head up. I felt so beaten down that it was sometimes difficult to walk. She then explained that I, like her, would not be doing anything by my own power, but I would be allowing God and the angels to work through me.

She told me that what we resist persists. She said that if I continued to push against negative energy and fight it as I had been, it would continue to push back harder against me, and the battle would grow fiercer. It was important to use the power of God's love instead of force. Since I have been back in the United States in the last year, I have heard this saying. However, back then it was the first time I had heard it, and this way of thinking was new to me.

I appreciated that she never forced her opinions upon me or manipulated me in any way. She did answer my questions and helped clarify things the angels told me that were at first completely beyond my understanding. These were entirely new concepts for me and very different than my former beliefs.

Mabel explained to me that on the earth, man is given free will. And to allow for maximum opportunities for our growth while on the earth, polar opposites exist—light and dark, front and back, good and evil, etc. One cannot exist without the other. All of these contrasts exist for a purpose. They help our souls to evolve and expand. In heaven none of these opposites exists. I understood what she was saying, but I did not yet entirely understand how significant this was. I was still feeling rather dazed.

She said that the angels told her that I needed to start meditating twice a day. Mabel said she would teach me how. I wasn't very interested in meditation. Nor did I understand the importance of it. I did see some benefit from the meditation I had previously practiced in Singapore, but I felt that I often just fell asleep. I was much more interested at that time in being free from the pressure in my head and having just a few minutes of relief from the pounding headaches. Mabel taught me how to meditate the next week. She was very persistent and called me every day to ask me if I had meditated, as it was crucial. Once I saw the benefits, it became a lifeline for me and became almost as necessary as breathing, especially in the following seven years. I explain how she taught me to meditate in the back section titled "Learning to Meditate Mabel's Way."

She reminded me to start trying to remember and write down my dreams as the angels would also be entering and working with me in my dreams and during my sleep. She asked me to keep a notebook and pen by my nightstand.

She told me that this was all for my highest good. I did not understand. I thought, *How can this possibly be for anything good? And what does that even mean anyway? Why me?* I was angry that I had all of this weird stuff by me. Mabel explained that our *highest good* are the events, lessons, and trials that we go through in our lives that keep us on our path to our souls' purpose. Often these things do not feel like they are good for us at all, but they are exactly what we need or what our souls have chosen. Mabel asked me to call her when I felt the time was right or if I wanted to see her again for another session.

I left the session feeling exhausted, shocked, slightly traumatized, but at the same time, amazed. I had a very deep knowing that what I had experienced was *real*. At the same time I knew it was all necessary and part of a bigger plan that I could not yet understand. I also felt profound love and joy from feeling the powerful love and light of God, Jesus, and the angels. I believe that this light stayed with me from that day on and something changed within me.

In addition, now I *knew* that God existed. I have believed that from the earliest time I can remember, and I have had many times in my life when I felt his love; however, now I knew that I knew that I knew. It is a completely different type of knowing when you have once seen someone or you feel like you met someone for the first time in person, especially if you have only been talking with the person on a phone with only occasional reception until that time. This was the same for me regarding St. Michael, St. Raphael, and the angels. Now I had seen them and met them, and there was no denying that what I had experienced was real or that these other realms existed.

It took a day or two for my physical and mental body to recover, and I needed extra sleep. The most wonderful part was that after I recovered a day, I had my normal energy back, I did not have the fever, and I could walk without pain. Most importantly I no longer felt that terrifying *evil* feeling I had felt the years before.

That evening I tried to tell Michael on the phone about what had happened to me in my first session and about the angels I had seen and the love of God that I felt, but he was not interested. I knew that I had experienced something incredible and profound that day. I did not want to tell him about the demons and the things regarding the lost souls, as that would be enough to freak almost anyone out. I never planned to tell anyone about all of the beings that had emerged from me that day, but now I feel called to, even if it somehow helps only one person. In recent years, I have heard several others who can see in the spiritual realms convey that they see similar beings with many people they encounter who are ill. They feel they are given the gift of seeing in the spirit to free the people of these dark entities and then the individual is healed.

My First Journey to Heaven

I went to see Mabel again the next week. I felt a strong *nudging* and a *knowing* that I needed to see her. I learned to trust and pay closer attention to those nudges more than I ever did. I felt so much better after the first session that I was very relieved and grateful. She commented that I also looked noticeably better! After we talked a short time, we began the hypnotherapy healing session. This was the first time I was taken to heaven. I was not expecting this, and neither was Mabel. What I experienced that day surpassed anything I could have possibly imagined.

There are no words to describe what I felt every time I was taken to heaven, but I will try my best to explain what I felt and saw. It was consistent and almost exactly the same every time, with only a slight difference in the intensity of the feelings, the brightness of the light, and the speed at which I felt I was ascending. From the moment that I saw the white light of God and felt the incredible unconditional love of God, I knew that I was going to my true home in heaven. I always understood that I was not there to stay. I also knew that I had not died.

The best way that I can begin to describe what I experienced is by saying that it felt like I was being carried straight up toward the sun rather quickly. Although I usually felt as though I was traveling fairly quickly, it did seem to take some time or I felt as though I had journeyed quite a distance. It was effortless, and it felt completely natural like I had done this many times before.

At first the light was golden yellow like the sun, and then the light changed to pure bright white the closer I got. Even though my eyes were closed, I instinctively raised my arms to shield them, thinking I might be blinded as the light became more and more intense. The joy was so overwhelming as I ascended that I could not help but laugh out loud with euphoric elation.

I was completely overwhelmed with a love that I cannot fully describe in words. I knew that this was the love of God. It was pure, powerful, infinite, and unconditional. The only way I can come close to describing the unconditional love of God is if I added up how much I loved my husband, daughter, and entire family and then multiplied the entirety of everyone I loved by an infinite number. To label it as infinite also seems inadequate, as this love has no limits and no bounds.

There simply are no human words to describe the unconditional love I experienced every time I journeyed to and was in heaven. I knew that it had no limits and it was eternal. And I knew at the same time that this was how much he loved every single one of us. God's love was not in any way exclusive.

The closest way I can describe the complete joy that I felt while I was ascending to heaven would be if I took the most joyful moments of my entire life and the most intimate moments of bliss and oneness I had ever experienced with my husband and then multiplied that by an infinite number. To multiply it times a hundred million would not be enough.

I believe that I have consistently known and received love throughout my lifetime. I felt very much loved by my parents and brothers and sisters while I was growing up. I felt very loved by my husband and his family, and I think I love our daughter as much as any mother loves her child. But the love I felt in heaven was a love of a much greater magnitude than I had ever felt before on the earth. I had only experienced glimpses or traces of this love until this time.

Meeting John Nicholas

When I arrived, I was immediately acknowledged by a group of about thirty people standing about twelve feet in front of me. They were standing in the shape of a triangle, arranged similar to bowling pins. I knew that these were my relatives. They didn't all come forward to happily hug and greet me as I later saw with every other soul who was welcomed into heaven. I think this was because they knew it wasn't yet my time to stay there. I felt that we all understood that this meeting was a privilege. Everyone seemed to respect this, and they all looked rather serious but still loving. A single man who was standing at the very front of the triangle of people came forward. He looked familiar, but I didn't know who he was. He was wearing tan pants and a cream-colored shirt. He seemed to emerge out of a white misty cloud as he came toward me.

He said, "Hello, my name is John, John Nicholas." Immediately I knew that he was my great-grandfather. I realized that it was the same John that briefly came forward during my first meeting with Mabel. Remarkably as soon as he said his name, I became one with him. I instantly knew everything about him. I knew what he loved and what he valued, and I felt his character. I saw images of the most important events of his life quickly flash before my eyes. I liked him a lot. He was very kind, rather soft-spoken, gentle, and funny like my dad. I knew that he also knew and understood me well just as I now knew him. I then felt the love he had for my dad. Then I felt the love he had for me. He told me he was happy that I came and that they were praying for this. He thanked me for coming. I understood how much we were connected, even though we had never met before. I had never even met my dad's parents, as they died before I was born. I knew that I was in exactly the right place at the right time. And I knew that this man had been faithful to God and that this was possibly why we were allowed to have this meeting. With this came an understanding that many of those who came generations before me had a great love for God and were faithful to God.

He said that he had important messages for me to give to my dad. He told me it was important for me to tell him these things as soon as possible.

He said, "Please tell him these messages face-to-face so he can see the truth in your eyes and hear the truth in your voice." He told me that my dad did not have very long to live and that it was very important that he received these messages and took them to his heart before he died.

He proceeded to tell me that my dad was feeling like a complete failure in his life. He felt this way because someone close to him had repeatedly told him this. He was also feeling very worn down by the circumstances of life, and because of this, he even questioned if he deserved heaven. He had suffered a lot in the last years, and it was taking a toll on his spirit and soul and causing him to lose hope. He thought he had possibly done something wrong to deserve this suffering.

He told me that it was imperative that my father understood that he deserved to go to heaven. And that he was not a failure. He wanted me to remind him of every good thing I could think of that he had done as a father and as a man. I needed to impress upon his heart the truth about how much he deserved to go to heaven. And I needed to tell him that he was worthy of heaven and that the truth was that he had not failed. He always did his best with what he had at the moment, and that was all that mattered. His intentions were consistently good. It was made known to me that this other realm I had seen the week before was possibly where my dad might be going if he was not clear about his deserving heaven.

I was asked to tell him how much God loved him and to say that God wanted all of his children to return home to heaven. This is not because we have done something to deserve this but because of his great mercy and what he has done for us.

I was supposed to tell him that when it came time for him to leave this earthly life, if the Devil came and tried to tempt him and shame him by showing him every way he had failed in his lifetime and tried to convince him that he was not worthy of going to heaven, he was supposed to call the name of God or Jesus and shoot like a rocket toward the light and heaven. Once he called the name of Jesus or God, he would be immediately escorted to heaven by the angels.

I was told to ask him to forgive himself. I was supposed to ask him to see himself through the eyes of God, his Father in heaven. God saw him as pure and innocent, and loved him unconditionally.

At this time I was then posing many questions to my great-grandfather. I thought, *How is this even possible? How did you find me? How does this work?* He explained it to me not in words but rather in feelings and visions. Throughout our entire conversation we were communicating telepathically—thought to thought, feeling to feeling, and soul to soul, without moving our mouths. It was easy and natural. It was like I had always done this. There was no room for misinterpretation this way. This was how the communication was with every being I ever encountered in the other realms.

He explained, "If your daughter had a child, wouldn't you love that grandchild?"

I thought, *Yes, without a doubt.*

He said, "If you saw that your grandchild was in trouble, wouldn't you do everything within your power to try to help him or her if you could?"

I thought, *Most definitely, yes!*

He said, "This is my opportunity!" He told me that my dad and I were both connected to him and that we were all connected in spirit.

I was given an understanding in this realm and a knowing that I had never experienced before. I knew this was not an accident or a coincidence. I knew that I was in exactly the right place and at the right time. I understood that I was part of a much broader group of souls and that I had a profound knowing that our souls were all much more intertwined and interconnected than I had ever realized or contemplated. I also felt that if this were the suffering I needed to go through to help a soul I loved, I would do it all over again. I felt that if I possibly could contribute in any way to helping my dad, then everything I had endured was all worth it.

The angels told me that this was an assignment and that it was my obligation. After the session Mabel also told me that I should do as they requested. I knew that she was right.

Even though what my great-grandpa had told me in heaven made perfect sense to me, and the entire experience was as real to me as anything on this earth plane, I still felt hesitant to tell him these messages. At the same time I knew that I had no choice.

My dad was named after his grandfather, and his name is also John Nicholas. He had been criticized and beaten down throughout much of his life by someone very close to him, and he was often made to feel like a failure, so I knew that part was all true. In the fifteen years prior to this time, he had suffered from a brittle bone disease and had experienced multiple fractures of his hips, legs, and back. The latest injury seemed to have taken the greatest toll on his body and spirit. My dad loved to weld and create needed inventions for the farm in his shed. A few years before this time a large piece of sheet metal had fallen from a high loft near the ceiling in his large machinery and work shed on the farm and landed on top of him, crushing his pelvis and tailbone. He was pinned under the weight of the heavy steel until my mom found him a few hours afterwards. He still had tremendous pain years later. I felt that this last accident literally crushed him in many ways.

My dad had incredible determination and strength. He was six feet tall and thin with broad shoulders and a natural six-pack. As a farmer, he had worked physically hard his entire life. There were several times that various doctors told him that he would never walk again, but he always managed to, even after this last accident.

My German wedding day, May 25, 1991, happened to also be his sixty-fifth birthday. He said to me during the father-daughter dance, "Today my prayers were answered." I asked him what his prayers were. He replied, "That I would be able to dance again!" He and my mom had always enjoyed dancing together throughout their entire marriage until his first injuries. My mom's name is Bonita, and so our neighbors and their friends referred to them as "Johnnie and Bonnie." In the sixty years that they were married, they had danced numerous polkas and waltzes together. When they danced, you could tell that they had many years of practice dancing together, as they were in perfect rhythmic unison. While growing up in rural Iowa, dancing was a big part of every major celebration, and it was something they enjoyed regularly as a couple from the night they first met, which was at a dance.

Johnnie and Bonnie at a wedding dance

My First Assignment from Heaven

A few weeks later on Christmas Day of 2004, I was able to see my dad and take him aside and deliver these first messages from his grandfather in heaven. I was uncomfortable to begin the conversation, even though the messages were so full of love and hope. It was just all so unbelievable that I was a little afraid that he might worry that I had lost my mind. My dad and I had often spoken deeply about our faith and our beliefs so this part was not unusual for us.

To my surprise and delight, when I told him what had happened and how I had met his grandfather in heaven and said that he had asked me to deliver some messages to him, he did not respond in disbelief. Instead he listened intently to every word I had to say. As I was instructed, I made a list of every good and successful thing that I could think of that he had ever done, and I read this to him. I especially thanked him for passing on his love for God and his strong faith to us, and I told him that this was the greatest gift he could have ever given his children. His eyes welled up with tears, and he started to cry. A big burden seemed to be lifted from his face. He was fascinated and wanted to know more. During the following days—and every time I was able to be home in the United States until he passed away—he enthusiastically asked me to tell him the story and repeat the messages over and over again. I wrote everything down for him so he could refer to it as often as he wanted.

When I finished speaking, my dad then spoke with great pride and told me more about his grandpa John (Johann) Nicholas Streit. He came to the United States as a young man from a poor farm near Erdorf, Germany. He was born in January of 1844. He paid $16.00 for a boat ride to the United States. When he arrived, the Civil War was taking place. He tried to enlist as a soldier, but he was not accepted because of an injury. He found work helping to build the transcontinental railroad line going east and west. When he had earned enough money to buy land, he traveled for weeks across unsettled prairie land with an ox-pulled cart and eventually found his dream of good farmland. He settled in northwestern Iowa in a small town called Ashton. He reportedly went to church daily, and church services were held in his home whenever there was a priest available. He helped build the town's first church on his land. He died in 1918 in Ashton.

Michael and I first visited this area where my great-grandfather was from in Germany in 1991. We were able to visit the village church and get a copy of the church records from the priest. These documents contained all of my paternal ancestors' names and important dates in them. The farms were very small, and the patches of hilly land were not suitable for farming. It was still apparent why he would have needed to leave, especially after numerous wars and famine. It was common for a few of the younger men to first travel to America and establish themselves before others in the family moved over. I later found a newspaper article about him that also included a picture of him, and it verified all of these things about him. It also said that he was known to be very hardworking and was quietly determined just like my dad. It mentioned all the difficulties he encountered as a settler in the Midwest, but that he did not give up his hope or his dreams.

Upon completion of this first assignment, I felt an incredible sense of fulfillment and a connection to heaven that I was not aware of before. I felt like the angels were speaking through me as I spoke with my dad. It initially felt very surreal but also really incredible. I did not yet know that this was the beginning of what would be part of my life path and soul purpose.

Shortly before my dad's death on October 23, 2010, at the age of eighty-four, my sister was with him and was able to remind him of all of the things that his grandpa had said that day. I also wrote him a letter that I felt was divinely inspired. It reminded him to shoot like a rocket toward the light and to call the name of Jesus or God if the Devil came and showed him all the ways in which he had failed and tried to convince him that he did not deserve heaven. I felt as though he took this message to heart and had complete peace during his passing.

We were incredibly moved when hundreds of people attended his wake and funeral. I believe this helped my mom a great deal with healing. The last years of his life were also not easy for her, as she had cared for him as long as she could with his multiple injuries and numerous trips to doctors and specialists over the last ten years of his life. I think what surprised me the most was how many young farmers from the county came to the visitation and wake. I had never met them before, but they encouraged me by telling me stories about how much they liked my dad and how he had helped and inspired them.

I have sung at many funerals, but this to me was one of the most beautiful I have ever attended, even as sad as I was. Of course, my view of death at this point had already changed greatly because I now had been in heaven. I knew that there was no reason to be sad for my dad, but I would still miss spending time with him on this earth. He was a great example of God's unconditional love and forgiveness. My aunts, uncles, and cousins provided lovely music while they sang in the choir. My cousin Gina has one of the most beautiful voices I have ever heard and her gifts of song were extremely moving. The songs the choir sang were the ones that I loved and grew up with. I am not sure if another can understand just how much it meant to me every time I could be in my hometown parish surrounded by the people that I loved after having lived so far away for so long.

My Dad's Welcome Party in Heaven

On the morning of his funeral I woke up with a vision of my dad flying like Superman toward the sky. He looked like he was around twenty to twenty-five years old. His back was straight, and his body was strong. I

95

had not seen him stand up straight for a few years. He had one fist pointed toward the sky. His straight brown hair was blowing with the wind as he was traveling very quickly toward the light. He had a great big grin on his face, and he looked very proud. This vision was so vivid that I was sure he had made it!

The day after his funeral I had a wonderful realistic dream of how he was welcomed into heaven. I was in that state when one is just about to wake up. It was like watching a beautiful clear movie screen up close and in HD. To me it was real, and it was a gift! There was a big celebration just for him. All of his relatives and friends were there, and they were all dressed in clothes from the early '50s. It was in an apple orchard. There were old-fashioned lights strung in the trees with medium-sized round bulbs. It was a beautiful summer evening. There was a four-and-a-half-foot-high white picket fence around the party with one section open in the front center. The other people faded into the background, and then my dad came to the open portion of the fence. I understood that I could not come into the fenced area where the celebration was. He was wearing casual pants and a white shirt. He had a great big grin on his face and appeared as if he had a secret he wanted to share with me. He held up a cup of what looked like the most refreshing beer I had ever seen. He said that there was a freshly tapped keg of beer and that it was the best beer he had ever tasted. As he held up the cup for me to look inside, I was able to taste it and it was the most refreshing beer I had ever sampled. After having lived in Germany for so long, I must have heard that song *In Heaven There is No Beer* dozens of times. I briefly recalled that song and thought, *Who said so?*

He asked me to thank my brothers and sisters for planning such a beautiful funeral. He especially thanked my one sister who had done most of the funeral arrangements. She had prepared everything with great love, honor, and respect. He wanted us to know that he had arrived in heaven and that he was really happy. He also thanked and acknowledged my younger brother John, who stayed with him a longer time before he died. John prayed with him and coached him at the end of his life. He also wanted to thank all of us for our prayers, love, and affection during his lifetime and in his last days.

This dream was so realistic to me that there was not a doubt in my mind he had made it. I remembered how much my dad enjoyed a good beer on a hot summer day and how much he loved socializing at family and community events. He also loved his apple trees. During the summer months, despite all the work there was to do, he always made sure that they were watered and cared for. So this seemed like it would be his perfect idea of what his first day in heaven and his welcome party would be like.

What struck me was how awesome it was that my dad's first experience of heaven was individualized in a way that fit him so perfectly. I had never considered this or thought that much about heaven before this time. But every time I saw a soul after their arrival in heaven, I continued to see this perfect alignment of what would most bring each newly arrived soul in heaven the most joy.

My dad John

Changed Forever

One thing I knew for sure after I was in heaven for the first time was that I was changed forever. I felt that life on the earth would never be the same. When I was in heaven, I was bursting with feelings of complete joy, happiness, fulfillment, and belonging. Now I was longing for these same intense and positive feelings on the earth. I seemed to be acutely aware of what was missing and the earth seemed particularly boring and meaningless in comparison. Now I believe it is exactly this separation from heaven and the love of God that our souls feel and try to fill in many ways while we are on the earth.

I had heard throughout my lifetime that God loves me unconditionally, and I believed it. But now I *knew* it in the very depth of my inner most being down to the very last cell.

There were so many things that were in truth different than my previous beliefs. Most importantly, that God was more loving, inclusive, forgiving, and merciful than I had ever imagined. And it was also very important that it was all about his righteousness and not my own. It was clear to me that it was never about me striving to be perfect with the hope of God accepting me. It was about God accepting me wholeheartedly, despite my imperfections and failings.

I was so overwhelmed by the unconditional love of God that I wanted to climb to the top of the highest mountain and shout out for the whole world to hear, "God loves you just as you are!" But I did not. I wanted so badly to share everything that I had experienced with everyone I loved, but my fear kept me silent. How could anyone believe this, as I could hardly believe what had happened myself? At the same time I knew I wasn't crazy. I knew that it was real. I have often been told throughout my life that I am very transparent and easy to read, but still I was afraid of this story not being accepted as genuine.

At the same time, I knew that nothing could ever take away or minimize what I had experienced and learned in heaven. I felt that everything I had ever learned from studying many hours of nutrition, biochemistry, medical terminology, and diseases in college could be easily forgotten. But what I experienced in heaven was etched into my heart, mind, and soul forever. Mabel explained to me that I could not learn in a classroom or by studying a thousand books what I had learned that day in heaven with the angels. The first time she said it, I thought that it was at least a slight exaggeration, but the more I continued to be taken to heaven, the more I realized that she was right.

It did not matter to me if some thought that heaven was a state of mind. I now knew that it was a real place. I feel that we are called to bring these same feelings that exist in heaven to the earth as much as we are possibly able.

CHAPTER

8

The Head Trauma

Mabel explained to me before this session that the healing process was similar to peeling an onion. I would be healed layer by layer until I would eventually get to the core. The most significant emotional wounds would be revealed to me first because they were affecting me the most.

During the next two sessions I was taken back to what were my two deepest childhood wounds. Growing up on a large farm, I experienced quite a bit of physical trauma as a child, and I remember several incidences and severe accidents very clearly. One of them was when I was eight years old and I fell off of the back of a tractor and onto the sharp wagon hitch. My right leg was split open at the knee. I am very lucky to still have both of my legs. Another was when I was drug down a gravel road by a galloping horse. However, the events I uncovered in these regression sessions were so traumatizing that I had completely blocked them from my memory. Today I remember them as if they happened yesterday. Again I would prefer not to mention them, but they are an important part of my journey. And I realize that I help no one by omitting them.

In the beginning of this hypnotherapy session it first appeared as though I was looking at our old black-and-white television when I was a young child and the antenna needed to be adjusted. The reception was poor and the image was fuzzy. Then suddenly all of the small black and white dots came together and formed the image of a nun. Everything then became clear and focused and changed into color. She was holding a brown wooden block, the kind we often used in music class. It was normally hit with a drum stick to make a percussive sound, and it was in the shape of a rectangle about three inches wide, ten inches long, and an inch deep. There was a cute little girl in a dress sitting on the school desk in front of her. I knew that she was very kind and sweet. I realized that this little girl was me, and I remembered wearing that dress. All of a sudden I became her. I knew that it was my first day of school. We were in the music room on the third story at the back of the school. She held me back after class and put me on top of the desk. The nun started speaking really mean to me. She scowled at me as she held her thin, wrinkled face close to mine. I noticed that she had an accent, discolored teeth, and stinky breath.

She then started beating me with the wooden block as hard as she could. At the same time she was yelling, "You are so stupid! Nobody loves you! You make me sick! You are so ugly! You are so fat! It's all your fault! Stop crying, or I'll hit you harder!"

Even at the age of six I knew that what she was saying wasn't true, and yet I believe that it went into my subconscious. I also knew that I did not deserve this and that what she was doing was wrong. She was hitting me on my shoulders, back, neck, and head, using all her force. The pain was incredible. I think she hit me around thirty times, each time purposely using the corner of the block for maximum pain. She told me to stop crying or she would hit me harder. I was screaming with my mouth shut. It seemed like it would never end. She threatened me and said that if I told anyone, she would beat me again and worse.

The next thing I was aware of was that I was in the bathtub at home and my mom was observing my back. I was above my body and was looking down at myself in the tub. It was as though I was wondering whether it was safe to enter my body again or not. Then I saw my mom as she analyzed my beaten back, shaking her head in disbelief. It was as if I could hear what she was thinking. I heard, *Oh, no! What happened?* My back and shoulders were covered with large black and blue bruises. There were even some open wounds. She asked me what happened, but I could not speak. I was in shock. She was horrified, but she was afraid to say anything, as she had several kids in the school and she didn't want to cause any trouble. One did not easily confront religious authority back then. I heard her reasoning in her mind back and forth. *Maybe she did something to deserve it.* She then thought, *I will wait and see if this happens again before I say anything.*

I experienced three more beatings that happened on Mondays after music class. All of these times were much worse, as the nun concentrated solely on hitting me on my head so there would not be any bruises or evidence. The pain was excruciating. I could not take it another second, and I thought I was going to die. The only way to escape and survive was to leave my body and disassociate. I then watched the nun beating me from several feet above my body. I do not remember seeing any angels or light. I know I needed to leave my body during at least three of the four beatings to survive the pain.

During the fourth time I came back into my body when she began molesting me. I was completely confused. I thought, *What is she doing to me? How is she spanking me on the inside of my body? Why does it hurt so much? How can I stop her?* I wished I were bigger and stronger so I could stop her. Even at the age of six I knew that what she was doing was very wrong. I was completely devastated and broken. I also could not understand how I could be sent back to school with no one to protect me. While she was molesting me, I saw the door open and the light come in. I was extremely relieved. I knew help had arrived. It was over. I believe she was sent away soon after that. I was taken back to the classroom sobbing and in shock. Everyone laughed at me. They couldn't have known.

I remained in shock for several days after each of the last three beatings. I did not want to go to school, and I pretended that I was sick and tried to stay in bed. I also did not want to wear a dress ever again. It was then that I first took comfort in singing and felt a connection with my angels. I also started praying. I developed a strong love for animals, especially our two farm dogs and many cats. I felt safe when I was with them as they were consistently loving and never mean. I also wanted to make myself bigger and stronger so that this could never ever happen again. This was when I started to gain weight.

Suddenly I was no longer the little six-year-old Karen, but I was brought back to the present time and was aware that I was in a hypnotherapy session. As I was in an altered state and in another realm, Mabel and the angels were always there in every session to comfort and to encourage me to forgive the nun so I could release the experience and be healed.

Almost instantly I had the image of the nun in the present time. She was very old and sitting in a wheelchair in a convent. I became one with the nun and then knew everything about her, and I could feel everything she was feeling. She was very weak, and she was praying for forgiveness. Her name was Agnes. Her parents were from Germany. Her mother did exactly this same thing to her many times. Her father was ill and did not know how to stop it. She told her repeatedly that she had never wanted her and finally sent her to the convent. Agnes had never wanted to be a nun. She just wanted to be loved. She was trying to relieve her own buried pain. She wanted to take my innocence as hers had been taken. Now she knew that she was going to die soon. Having this knowledge and understanding did help me to have empathy for her and to forgive her. Mabel was somehow observing all of this with me and coached me through forgiving her.

Following this session, although I knew what I had just relived was real, it took me a several years to process it and accept it. It is only in the last year that I can verbalize what happened to me and now write about it. I only recently feel that I have been fully healed. During this last year I have received traditional psychotherapy for the first time in my life and feel that I completed the last of the healing in regards to these injuries, the extreme trauma and abuse of the most recent years, and the limiting beliefs that I acquired because of them. As my therapist said to me, I survived everything up until this time. I get an A+ for survival in my lifetime. But what these experiences left me with are beliefs about myself that are not true, especially regarding my self-worth and the amount of shame and pain that I was carrying. So she helped me to replace these beliefs with more truthful beliefs. She is an excellent psychologist and I am grateful I had the opportunity to work with her. I wanted to assure that I did not continue to carry any of this with me as I feel I have carried it long enough.

I had sometimes wondered why I could not remember certain years of my life and who my first-grade teacher was. I had often felt like something major had happened to me and was still affecting me, but I had no idea what. The following school year my mom took us all out of our school, and we went to public school in a different town for the first week. I did not know anyone. I always thought that it was because of the tornado, but this made me wonder if this possibly also played a role in her decision, even if it was on a subconscious level. If I remember correctly, the nuns asked her if we would come back to the school in Stacyville, and I was glad to be back with my friends at our original school.

As unfortunate as it was and as extremely sad as I was for the little Karen, it was like being given a giant piece of a puzzle that I had been searching for the last years of my life. It explained why I was having the recurring headaches and pressure in my head. It also explained why after the incident with the brain injury, the German doctor was so upset about all of the abrasions on my head and was very adamant that I find out what they were from. It was as though it was continually coming up and revealing itself so that it could finally be healed. After this session I never had this pain or pressure in my head again. I now had clarity, focus, and peace. Now it all made sense. The pieces of the puzzle were coming together. I realized that healing could only occur when I discovered the truth.

I was shown that God did not cause me to suffer. He does not want any of his children to suffer. I chose these things as a way of forcing the expansion of my soul so that I would reach my true soul purpose in this lifetime. However, I would not recommend head and brain trauma to anyone. I realize that I am fortunate that I was not affected in many more ways, and I am extremely grateful that I have been able to function as well as I have all these years despite the head injuries. I believe this may only be because of my parent's constant praying for their children. I am counting on heaven to keep my brain functioning well until the end of my days.

On a nicer note, it also possibly clarified some other things. I sometimes felt that I received favor from the nun who was the principal at the grade school. She was especially nice to me, and I sometimes wondered why, as she was not known for this. I seemed to win several coloring and painting contests in the second through sixth grade, even when I felt that someone else's was possibly better than mine. I remember it very well, so I know that it meant a lot to me back then, even if it was only receiving a sticker and a little recognition. There were several times when the nuns hung up my pictures or I was asked to go around to the various classes and read a humorous story I had written. Now I believe she was the same one that opened the door and ended the abuse that fourth Monday of the school year when I was in the first grade in 1970.

One other happy memory I have was when my mom surprised me with a wonderful cake at school that year on my seventh birthday, which was five months later. It was in the shape of a long train, cleverly decorated with tootsie rolls and lifesavers. There was enough for all thirty-two children and the teacher. I have a picture of myself proudly holding up the cake. It is still one of my favorite pictures from my childhood, as I am beaming with pride. The following fall I had a wonderful teacher named Mrs. Blake. She was very kind and gentle, and I felt very safe.

The Near-Death Experience

The next hypnotherapy session revealed a near-death experience that I had when I was three years old. It was a hot summer day in 1967. I saw myself as a little girl playing by a puddle of rainwater on the lane that was near our hay shed. The shed was quite far from the house. I then became the little girl Karen, and I knew that I was three years old. I then saw a boy with straight light brown hair standing next to me. From my view the sun was almost directly above him, so his shiny hair was reflecting the bright sun and I could hardly see his face. There wasn't a cloud in the sky. He asked me if I wanted to play with him, and he put out his hand. I took it, and he led me to the hay shed. There were two other boys there as well. One of them was distantly related to me, and the other two were his cousins, visiting from another state. They were fourteen, fifteen, and sixteen years old. The sixteen-year-old, who had led me into the shed, suddenly bent me over on a stack of bales and started raping me. The pain was incredible, and I was screaming and crying. The straw against my skin also hurt. As I was crying and screaming so much, he took off his white T-shirt and wrapped it around my face and head to stop anyone from hearing me. Because I was crying so much, my nose and mouth were already congested. Now that they were completely covered and his shirt was pulled tightly around my face, I could not breathe, and I was suffocating. I lost consciousness. All of a sudden I was about eight feet above my body, and I was very scared. I was panic-stricken and did not know what to do.

My spirit left my body and quickly went to my mom, who was in the kitchen of our house, busily cleaning up after a big meal. I could feel that she was worrying about all the work she had to do. I screamed, "Help me!" But she could not hear me. Although I realized she could not hear me, I was still hoping somehow she would. She did briefly look out the kitchen window toward the lane and think about me, hoping I was okay. There were so many kids to look after and so much work to do. We had extra men working on the farm that day, helping to bale the hay.

Then I was again watching everything from about eight feet above my lifeless body. I looked at the boy hurting me, and then it was as though I was briefly *one* with him. I felt how he just wanted to relieve his raging teenage hormones. I understood his character, which was lacking in morals and goodness. Then I quickly flashed forward into the present time and saw this boy, now a man working at his desk. I did not like him at all. He was miserable, as he was now reaping what he had sown throughout his entire life.

I was searching for someone to help me. So I then left his spirit and looked at the fourteen-year-old, and then I was suddenly one with him. I felt how he was scared and shocked and wanted his brother to stop. His fear intensified now that I had stopped moving. He was a good kid, and he knew that what his brother was doing was wrong, but he was afraid of him. Then I jumped forward to the present time and saw that this boy, who was now a grown man, still felt guilty and ashamed about what he had witnessed that day. He still wished he could have somehow stopped him. He was a good man, and I felt empathy for him. I somehow left his energy and was again above his body.

I looked at the next boy. Then I was *one* with the fifteen-year-old. I didn't like him at all. He was nervously laughing and watching out for my dad who was feeding the cows in the distance by the silos. I fast-forwarded in his life and saw that he was not a good man when he was older. I was shown how he also hurt other people very close to me.

All of this took place very quickly. Again, in this realm that I was in when I left my body, it was as though there was no time and I could easily move in and out of everyone's energy and go backward and forward in time very quickly with no effort. I was not trying to do any of this; it was as though my spirit followed my thoughts. My thoughts were trying to find help.

I screamed again, *"Help!"* Suddenly an angel appeared. Her name was Gloria. She looked like she was around twenty-five years old, and I knew that she was very wise. She was the most breathtakingly beautiful being I had ever seen. She was divinely lovely. When she was close, her face looked like a porcelain doll with big loving eyes. At this time they looked extremely concerned, and I felt her urgent desire to help me. She had very long locks of strawberry blond hair, and it was flowing as if we were underwater. When she moved quickly, she was transparent, leaving only an outline of her body. She was wearing a lustrous amber and copper-colored gown like the angels in Renaissance paintings. Her gown was also flowing. She said earnestly, "Stop. You have to go back!"

I said, "But I can't. I can't breathe! Help me!" She quickly disappeared, and I knew that she went to get my dad.

The next thing I remember, I was hanging upside down while my dad held tightly onto my legs with one arm against his chest, pounding on my back with the other hand, which was formed into a strong fist. After I began to breathe, he held me in his arms and carried me to the house and handed me to my mom, who put me in the bathtub. I saw blood running down his arm where I had been. There was only two inches of water in the tub. This was just like my mom, always conserving everything. She had been born in 1930, the year the Great Depression began. The water was mixed with blood. It was a hot summer day, but I was shivering, shaking, and freezing. My parents were discussing what might have happened to me. They were thinking that maybe I fell and landed on top of a fence post or a sharp rock. I understood that they could not even imagine what that boy had done, so I did not blame them. I did not understand it myself or have the words to describe it, and I could not speak. I only knew that he had hurt me, and I knew that it was wrong. I did not understand why he had hurt me. I could hear my mom thinking to herself that she would bring me to the doctor if the bleeding didn't stop. Back then we only went to the doctor if it was really necessary, as this was how my mom was raised. At this time I really wished that someone would have known what had happened and had comforted the little Karen more. I could see how desperately she needed it and how often this was missing.

As Mabel was somehow able to experience most of what I was reliving in the session, she asked to speak with the little Karen to see how she was doing now. I then met the little Karen again as the adult Karen. She was still afraid and fearful about what might happen to her next. She looked very sad and like she wanted to cry. Mabel tried to convince her that she was going to be all right and that no one would ever hurt her again. However, she was very smart. As she was in another realm, she could already see what was to follow, including the beatings from the nun when she was six years old. She asked Mabel how she could say that no one would ever hurt her again, as she could already see the beatings, the other traumas, as well as the pain and abuse that the adult Karen would continue to suffer. So there was no convincing her at this point that everything was going to be okay and that she would be safe from then on. As much as I wished that the little Karen would be convinced that she was safe and could be happy again, I realized that the stubborn and smart side of the little Karen most likely helped her to survive. Mabel talked with her some more and tried to cheer her up by hugging her, telling her how much she was loved, and giving her a red balloon.

All of a sudden three angels appeared and comforted me, now again as the adult Karen. They showed me that when this boy or the nun violated me and sinned against me in this way, my soul had been fragmented or broken into pieces. This was the broken feeling that I was experiencing. They showed me that even if it was only a crack in my soul, it was enough to allow darkness inside. It was imperative that all of these cracks in my soul from emotional wounds be healed so that no darkness could enter. I now knew that all of the darkness could be driven out of my soul by using the light and love of God. I felt that they were revealing to me that any person, if sinned against or violated even in a much lesser way, could potentially acquire cracks in their souls, or their soul could become fragmented.

In order for healing to occur, Mabel asked me if I would forgive these boys. Because I understood that it was imperative for myself, I tried my best to do this. She explained to me that in forgiving them, I was not condoning what they had done or agreeing that it was all right. I would be forgiving them on a soul level so that my soul could be free from this hurt and they could be released.

After I agreed to forgive them, it was as if I saw my soul coming together and being made whole. Again it was like various pieces of a puzzle coming together, except these pieces looked as though they had been ripped apart and were jagged and torn.

When this session was over, it took me at least thirty minutes to come out of this deep state. Once again Mabel told me that this was all for my highest good. I still wondered, *How can this possibly be for anything good?* I still did not understand what she meant by this. Many concepts she or the angels presented to me took more than one explanation for me to fully understand.

I was again shocked and saddened after this session. It took me a long time to accept something I knew was true. I was physically bleeding for a while after this session as verification that it was true. I had often wondered if I had been raped, but I thought, *I would definitely remember that.* Sometimes when I would look at a picture of myself when I was a child, I would think, *What happened to you?* I had recently even started having dreams about it, but I did not want to believe it or take it seriously. I then understood why I kept waking up in a panic, feeling like I was suffocating. After this session this did not ever happen again. As this was so frightening, I was very thankful for this reason alone that this was now resolved. My hay fever was also not nearly as severe as it had been before.

As horrible as it was and as much as I knew that this had affected me negatively throughout my lifetime, I knew that it was also a piece of the puzzle that I needed so that I could be healed. At least now I was getting the answers I had been searching for. They just were not any of the answers that I had even considered. Most importantly I knew that I was being healed.

I can still see that lovely angel's face as clearly today as I did that hot summer day in August when I was three years old in 1967. She is the first of my guardian angels I ever met. Her name, Gloria, had come to me so often in prayer in prior years, but I did not know if this really could be of any significance. I have seen her several times since that session. There are no earthly words to describe her beauty, as there is nothing on the earth as beautiful as she was. The only thing I ever saw in heaven more beautiful than her was Jesus and his mother, Mary.

From what I understood from the angels, it was these two incidences, as horrible and as tragic as they were, which helped to define who I was at a very young age. I was shown that these two traumatic events put me in alignment for fulfilling my life purpose and mission. It also gave me a great amount of empathy and compassion for abused children and anyone suffering. I also gained a great desire to help hurting people if I was ever in a position to do so. Presently my dream is to help build shelters for abused women and children.

As I mentioned previously, I only recently had my first sessions with a psychologist who had more than thirty years of experience with abuse. I decided to seek counsel and healing not because of these childhood incidences but because of the most recent abuse and trauma that my daughter and I had experienced, which was much worse. As we also addressed these childhood issues, she felt that disassociating would be a necessary response to survive. She also voiced that what was done to me was evil, and it would therefore be quite normal to feel an evil presence, as these things were trying to emerge to be recognized and healed. This unresolved childhood abuse attracted abuse as an adult so that I would finally resolve and heal these incidences. It may have also explained why I had such poor energetic boundaries.

After these two sessions my perspective changed regarding healing. Everything I had just learned in the two sessions when I was regressed contradicted what I had learned throughout my college education. We were taught that anything outside of Western medicine was quackery. Now I learned that my emotional wounds were making me physically sick, which was completely opposite from what I had been taught, which was twenty years prior to this. This caused me to reconsider my approach to healing. I believe that Western medicine is essential and saves many lives. But there is also a time and a place in instances like mine where traditional medicine could not heal my emotional wounds. Then, alternative therapy is necessary. So I believe it depends on what the root cause of the illness or pain is. My belief now is that the origin of many illnesses is unresolved emotional wounds.

That being said, I also learned over the years that what might be a wonderful healing experience or method for me may not be suited for another. The individual must be ready to accept healing and to work on any issues if needed. I cannot force anyone to be healed or to accept healing energy from me or from anyone else. From what I understand, it is always appropriate to pray for another in need and send healing energy, but the person's soul can still choose not to accept it if he or she is too proud, not willing, or not ready. Every person has free will and every person is on his or her own individual healing journey.

Me when I was 3 years old

CHAPTER

My Second Journey
to Heaven

Ask, Ask, Ask!

I believe that this journey to heaven was my most profound experience in heaven of all. I received a visitation from Jesus, Mary, and Joseph, and I had an intimate meeting with God. I feel it was also during this trip that I was given some of the most important information that I am now called to share with as many people as I possibly can.

Again I was with Mabel, lying on a bed and having a hypnotherapy session. I was taken to heaven again for learning. This journey to heaven was almost exactly the same as my first one. I felt like I was being quickly but gently carried toward the sun. Initially the light was a bright golden yellow. As I ascended, it changed to a bright white light. The light was intense and became brighter and brighter, so much so that I shielded my closed eyes with my arms crossed over my face, thinking that I might be blinded. I was overwhelmed with pure, powerful, infinite, and unconditional love. I knew that this was the love of God. It was as if this love penetrated every cell of my body. There is no earthly way to measure this love, as it is infinite. The joy was immeasurable. I cried for joy and laughed out loud. It was the greatest bliss I had ever known. I knew that I was going to heaven, and I knew that it was my true home.

When I arrived, I was sitting up on a brass bed with my back resting against the headboard, and I was tucked in with a soft pink blanket. I felt very safe. I looked like I was around fifteen years old. I knew that this was my highest self. I was wearing a long white nightgown exactly like the one my sister Mary gave me when I was that age. It was pure white and silky on the outside and soft on the inside. There were three angels standing next to my bed on the right. They were beautiful, pure, and very wise, and appeared to be around fifteen years old too. Their faces were flawless and looked as though they were made out of porcelain. They had medium-length shiny golden blond hair with some locks and flips on the ends. They were each wearing simple white shiny gowns.

They were completely delighted to see me. They were so happy that they were giddy with laughter and joy. They were thrilled that we were together again and that I had asked for help. They said, "It's so nice to see you again!" I initially thought to myself, *again?* But, then I realized that they were right. I felt the most incredible unconditional love. It was as though we had known one another forever and they knew everything about me. They loved me with the same unconditional love of God, and they saw me through his eyes. In their eyes I was perfect, whole, and complete just as I was. Although I knew that they knew all of my human faults, it all did not matter, as there was no judgment. They loved and treasured everything about me. They asked me to try to love myself as God loved me now that I could see how he loved me through their eyes.

All communication was telepathic. I knew their thoughts and feelings, and they knew mine. If I understood rightly, they were learning from me while I was learning from them. This is how the communication was every time I was together with God, the angels, or any being in heaven or in these other realms. It seemed completely natural and easy.

They told me to keep asking! "Ask, ask, ask," they said. They said that it did not matter how big or how small my need was, whether it was colossal or minute, I should ask in all circumstances. They said that it gave them tremendous joy to help me, as it in turn brought joy back to God because we are all *one* in truth. They told me that I could never ask for too much or ask too often.

Then they shared many messages with me. The biggest message they had for me was this: "Please take better care of yourself!" They began by asking me to extend the same kindness, forgiveness, and non-judgment to myself that I easily gave to others. They told me that I was consistently putting myself last on my list of priorities. I was too often denying my own needs and taking care of everyone around me, and completely ignoring my own feelings and happiness. I was spreading myself too thin. I often said *yes* because I felt guilty or obligated and not because I really wanted to. They told me that one of the greatest gifts to offer my heavenly Father was healthy self-care and self-love. They shared with me that loving, honoring, and accepting myself was one of the greatest gifts I could give to God, as I was in truth *one* with him. When I did these things, I returned love, honor, and acceptance back to God. They asked me to work on accepting and loving myself as I was. And they asked me to remember that I was wonderfully and fearfully made in God's image.

Jesus, Mary, and Joseph—Every Prayer Is Heard

All of a sudden I saw the holy family on the left side of the bed that I was sitting up on. They were about one foot from the brass footboard. Mary was seated in the middle on a simple queen's throne. Jesus was standing to the right of Mary, and Joseph was left of her and kneeling on one knee. There was so much light emanating from them that I could not tell if they had halos or if it was the intense light reflecting from their hearts and heads. During one brief moment the light radiating from them had a green tinge on the end of the rays of light. I now knew that the color green symbolized healing. It was the same emerald green color that I saw every time when Archangel Raphael was present.

Jesus was wearing a pure white floor-length robe. His eyes emanated so much love and compassion. I had never seen such beautiful eyes before. Nor had I felt so much love coming from one individual. Mary was even more beautiful than the angels I had already met. There are no words to describe her beauty, as there is no one on the earth as beautiful as she was.

She was clothed in a simple long white gown and cloak. Her hands were resting on her lap. She was holding a golden scepter in one hand and a small golden globe in the other. I felt immense love, joy, peace, and pure feminine strength exuding from her. Joseph was in the traditional robe of his day, which looked like it was made out of tan linen or burlap. He had a staff in one hand and was kneeling on one knee. The other foot was flat on the floor in front of him. He was wearing sandals. He portrayed pure masculine strength, loyalty, and honor. I could feel how much they all loved me and how much both of the men loved, honored, and adored Mary.

They collectively had one main message for me. "We hear your prayers!" This was their big message for me and for all of mankind. They hear our prayers every time we pray. They revealed to me that heaven is just waiting for us to *ask*. On earth mankind has been given free will, so they cannot intervene, except in some life-threatening situations and it is not yet our time to go, unless we ask. Ask and then surrender your prayers to them and then *trust*. Then meditate, listening for instructions as to the steps needed to take in the right direction. And then move in that direction one step at a time.

They also said that they were constantly watching over me. I had asked them consistently, and they said that they came the first time I asked.

This is why a visitation from the holy family was so significant to me. As I mentioned earlier, my sister and I had begun saying a novena simultaneously to the holy family several years before this for our family. It was my sister's idea. With such a big family, there were always many prayer needs. I continued to say this novena for my own family and prayed to them almost every day while I was sick. As stated earlier, a novena is a set of prayers that is said every day for a specific number of days for a particular prayer request.

Suddenly about twelve feet directly in front of me was the apostle Saint Jude Thaddeus. He was wearing a white robe with a green shawl. He portrayed pure hope and faith. I have said novenas to him since I was a teenager, as he is known to be the patron saint of miracles for those with hopeless cases and lost causes. I had translated and distributed his prayers many times wherever we lived in the world, and he thanked me for this. Depending on which theology you believe, he was a cousin or close relative of Jesus and the brother of the apostle James and wrote a book in the Bible.

I know that there was at least one other person standing in the corner of the room behind the holy family. However, I could not tell who it was because of the great amount of light that was radiating from them. I believe it was a small group of other saints that I had often prayed to.

The three angels standing to the right of me asked if I had any questions that I wanted to ask the holy family or St. Jude. They encouraged me and told me that I could ask anything I wanted. I was awestruck and speechless. I thought, *Who? Me? Who am I to ask any of you questions?"* All of a sudden my heart blurted out three questions, and they heard it. The first was, "What have I done wrong to deserve all of this suffering?" The second was, "If you have heard my prayers and you're constantly watching over me, then why was I sick for so long, and why did I have to experience so much evil?" And the third was, "Why can't I just be normal?" I just wanted to be normal. I then had all of these questions completely and thoroughly answered.

At a Table Together with God—My Life Purpose

Immediately I was brought to a different place that was completely white. I was seated together with God at the most beautiful table I have ever seen. It looked as though it was a cross section of a very large ancient tree and was about six feet long, four feet wide, and four inches thick. There was every beautiful shade of wood tone that one could possibly imagine, ranging from a dark rich mahogany and ebony to the lighter tones of alder and ash, all alternating within one piece of wood. Each irregular ring in the table was a different shade and kind of wood, but all were present in one perfect piece of wood. This is just one example of what I would later see in heaven. I saw many things that completely defied the laws of nature and logic on the earth, and that make it difficult to comprehend and explain. There was a thick layer of clear crystal or diamond or something similar on top of the wood that made the table very shiny.

God was seated directly kitty-corner across from me and to my left. I knew immediately that it was him. I could not see his face, as there was so much light emanating from him. He looked like a big oval-shaped cloud of pure glorious energy. I felt the most overwhelming *fatherly* unconditional love that I have ever felt and will ever feel until I return. I knew that he wanted me to see my true magnificence. It was as though I could see myself for the first time as he saw me, and I was a million times more significant to him than I had ever imagined. I was magnificent! I understood that this is how he saw every one of his children. We are all magnificent in truth!

I knew that he knew me since the very creation of my soul, which was much older than I had ever imagined. I knew that he loved and adored everything about me just as I was. His love for me was pure and unconditional. I understood that I had not earned this love. Nor could I do anything to deserve it or to change it. This was God's love for me and for every one of us, each of his creations.

I knew that this was he and I sitting down together to talk before I reincarnated to the earth for this life I am presently living.

God asked me, "Where do you want to go? What do you want to do?"

I answered, "What do you want me to do?"

He solemnly replied, "Help my lost souls!"

With this, immediately God took me to a different gray place and showed me the lost souls. I reveal more about what I experienced in this realm in the chapter titled "The Lost Souls."

It was imprinted upon my heart how much God loves all of his children equally and how he had created them all. He is the only Creator in the entire universe, and in truth, we are all one with him and with one another.

Then, this concept of oneness with our Creator was expanded upon and broadened. It was as though I was one with him and he was one with me. It was even shown to me that because he exists everywhere, it is as if I have his DNA—not just me, but every one of us. Because he is everywhere, he exists in every part of our being, every cell, our very DNA. And this immense unconditional love was what he felt for every one of his children regardless of whether they accepted him as their Father or not. He said, "Many of my children do not accept me or acknowledge me, but still my love and mercy for them remains."

He said to me, "You love your daughter very much, right?"

I replied, "Yes, you know that I do."

He asked, "Is there anything she could possibly do that would keep you from loving her?"

I replied, "I don't think so."

He continued by saying, "Even if she disappointed you and hurt you, you would still love her because she is your child, right?"

I answered, "Yes, of course."

God said, "How many times would you want her back if she turned away from you or disappointed you?"

I said, "I think every time ... as long as I live."

He said, "*Yes, exactly!*"

It was then impressed upon my heart that I must take this tremendous love I had for my daughter and multiply it by an infinite number to even come close to his love for each of us. To even define it as *infinite* seems inadequate, as the love I felt in heaven from God had absolutely no limits, no bounds, no conditions, and no end.

God impressed upon my heart his desperate longing for each and every one of his children to return home to him. He wants them to understand their true magnificence and power through him. In saying that, I also feel I was given the understanding that without God I am nothing. But when I keep him in my life and stay in close relationship with him, I am never without him. And therefore, I am never without his almighty power, infinite love, mercy, grace, and abundant blessings.

I was shown that I had been asked to be a bridge between heaven and earth, those living on the earth and those who had crossed over into heaven, and this other realm between heaven and earth. I had volunteered for this or had agreed. It was a sacred contract.

At this point I felt I was given the opportunity to annul the agreement that I had made before my birth to do this work, as the spiritual torment I was enduring was sometimes more than I could bear. However, I felt that if I did this, I would be disappointing God, and I did not want to disappoint him. I also felt that my soul really wanted to complete this assignment. This work would be the summation of what I had worked for and done in many of my past lives. In addition, now that I understood more about past lives and soul purposes, I honestly did not want to take the chance that I might possibly want to come back and repeat all of this in a future life. So I consented again.

In observing my soul or highest self together with God at that extraordinary table, I noticed how much my personality is exactly the same today as it was then. If God asked me the same question today, I am certain I would answer in exactly the same way. It sounded exactly like something I would say.

I Chose It All

With this, I was taken back to the first room, where I was together with the three angels and sitting up comfortably on the brass bed. I was shown by the angels how everything I had experienced in this lifetime I had chosen or volunteered for to prepare me for my true life's mission, which was helping these lost souls, helping others to heal, and teaching and sharing what I learned in heaven.

They told me that I was not being punished in any way for something I did wrong. They wanted to make this very clear, for that was the first of the three questions that my heart had asked.

They explained to me that because I had chosen it all, the one that I needed to forgive the most was myself. Because every person is connected and even *one* in truth with the divine Father, the main one to forgive was myself. In forgiving myself, I forgave them.

They asked me to extend the same forgiveness, love, and kindness to myself that I easily gave to others. They told me that I often treated complete strangers kinder than I treated myself. I was not given a life on the earth solely to serve others or to be a sacrificial lamb but also to enjoy my life. It is wonderful, good, and necessary to serve others, but I was out of balance and felt guilty when I enjoyed my life.

I had a false sense of responsibility, meaning I felt I was solely responsible for the happiness and well-being of everyone close to me. They assured me that although it is wonderful to bring happiness to others, everyone is ultimately responsible for creating their own happiness. They told me that if I stayed in balance and made sure that my needs were met first, I would ultimately be able to serve others better and would have more to give to those I loved.

I was shown that in heaven, it is only possible to experience love, joy, peace, hope, and all the other most positive emotions. On earth we have the opportunity to experience all of the contrasting negative emotions, such as hate, fear, despair, and sorrow. I chose in this lifetime to experience many aspects of love in all of its varying degrees and contrasting opposites. By experiencing such tremendous fear, betrayal, abandonment, and even hate while on the earth, I would gain a much deeper understanding of the complete polar opposite, namely God's pure and infinite unconditional love.

In addition, by experiencing a shattered and broken heart while on the earth, I could more fully comprehend the fullness of heart I felt in the presence of God.

They revealed to me that I have a gift of knowing how to help people and what they need. This is a gift commonly born to people who are healers. However, when I continuously dive in and help people close to me by cleaning up or covering up their messes, I actually rob their souls of their life lessons and delay or inhibit their souls' growth. I should stop jumping in and rescuing people and intervene only when someone asks me and then only agree to help if it brings me joy to do so.

Suddenly I was again with the three different angels that were larger, more mature looking, and even wiser. We were watching my soul in heaven as it prepared to return to earth for this lifetime. I saw that I had a much bigger role than I had previously realized in planning my lifetime. I chose together with God, my angels, and spirit guides the major soul lessons, people in my life, triumphs, as well as trials. I already knew that at any given moment of my life and especially in the darkest and most difficult times, there would be someone there to help me through, even if it usually seemed to be at the very last moment. These people, whether a sister, a friend, a soul-mate, or a healer, were all chosen, and it was all planned before my coming to the earth for this lifetime.

I also saw how everything and everyone were part of one another and how it all fit together like a perfectly designed jigsaw puzzle. Everything was divinely orchestrated. My soul knew that I needed to choose such traumatic events in my lifetime to get to where I needed to be in order to fulfill my life purpose. As tragic as these events were, they helped define who I was at a very young age. I acquired an incredible amount of empathy for children and all hurting people because of the abuse and I needed this empathy to fulfill my soul purpose.

I understood that when I was suffocating and nearly died as well as when I was beaten and disassociated from my body, this connected me with heaven and opened the doors to these spiritual realms at a very young age. I believe it is possible with prayer and meditation to enter these realms without suffering, but this is the path my soul chose as a form of accelerated learning to make certain I would reach my life's mission.

In addition, as my soul really wants to help others to heal, the healer strives to acquire the necessary skills, and therefore always needs to heal him or herself first. *Practice* really does make *perfect* when it comes to healing.

As I understood it, every soul is born with the gifts they need to fulfill their mission or soul purpose. And, every soul has a purpose. Every purpose is important and needed. Everyone has the capacity to heal. These gifts may need to be practiced and refined, but they are present when we are born. The biggest clues as to what your life purpose is are found in where your greatest interests, passions, enthusiasm, and talents are and what brings you the most joy! When you begin to function in your soul purpose, heaven will open doors that you never dreamed possible. It is like a train that is finally on the right track and there is no turning back.

One thing that became very clear to me was that there is a purpose in everything that happens and there are no coincidences.

They asked me to keep singing, as there were healing properties in my singing and speaking voice. They asked me to sing whenever I had the opportunity, as my voice reached into the depths of people's hearts and souls and helped to heal them. Archangel Gabriel would be with me to help me communicate effectively, whether speaking or singing. They said the healing properties would continue to increase the older I became.

They told Mabel that my physical body was similar to a Maserati car and it was highly sensitive and required small amounts of pure fuel packed with the highest nutrients possible. Mabel encouraged me to follow their advice.

When we finished with this session, it again took me at least thirty minutes before I could open my eyes, and it took longer until I could move. Mabel said, "Wow, when you came to my house the first time, I thought you were just an ordinary woman with the usual problems and you would have *normal* sessions." She said very enthusiastically, "You have a lot to do!" She repeated, "You have a lot of work to do! You have a very big mission! You will be very busy!" I guess neither of us had expected any of this. I believe this was the first time that Mabel told me that I was being asked to write a book about these experiences. The idea seemed so unrealistic and far-fetched.

Honestly I wasn't thrilled when Mabel told me that I had a lot of work to do. I felt I had heard that almost my entire life from about the time that I could walk. To this day I can still hear my mom's voice in my head saying, "Put some elbow grease into it! If there's a will, there's a way!" I appreciate that this learned determination pulled me through many of the toughest times and that we were taught to work really hard and be very responsible when we were growing up. This has served me well throughout my lifetime. I also feel I developed a grateful attitude from having so little when I was younger. But right then I was still exhausted from fighting the spiritual battle, not sleeping enough, and the long illness.

At the same time various emotions were simultaneously running through my being. I was awestruck, amazed, shocked, and bewildered. I still had to think, *Who? Me? Why me?* So much of what I now knew to be the truth was different than what I had previously believed. Everything I learned in heaven became my new truth, as there was no denying the information when it was God and the angels that had presented it to me. It all resonated deep within my soul as absolute truth. There was not a doubt in my mind that everything I had experienced was real. I knew that I was there for learning, and I knew that I was supposed to share this information with others.

I also wondered what my soul was possibly thinking that I had agreed to do this kind of work. Why did I think I could do this? Why did God think I could do this? Why would I choose work that involved elements that frightened me so much? God obviously had much more confidence and trust in me than I had in him.

I also couldn't help but wonder if he had gotten me mixed up with one of my siblings. I had sometimes considered myself to be a notch below their level of intelligence, which was okay with me, as I still did all right for myself. But because I had such a difficult time accepting all of this and believing that I was good enough, I was taken many more times to heaven for further explanation and clarification. I learned that it had nothing to do with me being worthy or good enough. It was not about my righteousness but about God's righteousness. It did have some to do with my big and kind heart, but I was shown repeatedly exactly why this was my assignment. To put it simply, I was asked to do a job, and I agreed.

During this session the angels had encouraged me to change my beliefs and behavioral patterns. They had revealed several ways in which I was limiting myself and therefore limiting how God could work through me. I am the only one who can be responsible to change my beliefs. It took me years to integrate these new beliefs, and some I am still working on. I feel it has been a process of two steps forward and then one step backward with a pause for integrating the new beliefs. Some of these limiting beliefs were engrained into my subconscious mind during my childhood. Others were developed over lifetimes or passed down through the generations.

There were several things that I learned in this visitation to heaven that only made sense to me several years later. For instance, at that point in my life, in 2005, I had never in my entire life until this point hated anyone or felt tremendous betrayal, abandonment, or a shattered heart that I was aware of. These things only occurred a few years later, beginning in 2009. I was given so much information that I did not yet realize I would only truly understand and need several years later.

I now saw life on the earth differently. I believe I felt much more in control of my life when I was a young adult than I did at this time in my life. After I was sick for so long and had given so much of my personal power away over the years, I began to feel as though I had less and less control. I thought my life was similar to riding on an inflatable raft down a rough rapid river. I felt forced to go with the flow and take whatever came my way, and the best I could do was to try not to tip over and drown. I realized with this session that much of my life was planned in advance as far as important people, soul lessons, and soul purpose. However, the outcome was more similar to being sketched in pencil than carved in stone. I could determine much of the outcome by changing my thoughts and beliefs about myself to align closer to God's thoughts about me. His plans for me were much greater than my plans for myself! He imagined much more goodness, happiness, and abundance in every way for my life than I currently was envisioning. I had become distracted and fearful in recent years.

After the second time I journeyed to heaven, I was slightly concerned about becoming dependent on this ultimate level of bliss, as I felt it was the greatest level of ecstasy that any human could possibly experience while still on the earth. At the same time I had a distinct knowing that every time I decided to see Mabel for a session, it was necessary and what I was called to do.

By this time I was completely fascinated by Mabel's skills as a healer. She made it very clear that she was only an instrument of God and was nothing without him. But I couldn't help asking her why, if I was able to experience such incredible and powerful healing sessions with her because of her tremendous gifts and ability to summon angels, were people not beating down her door and begging for a session. I knew that she had many clients and was very busy with her healing practice. But I felt if more people knew about her capabilities, they would be lined up for miles waiting for a chance to encounter angelic beings and to visit heaven. She then told me that my sessions were not the typical sessions that other people underwent. Her other clients had not gone to heaven, and only some had seen traces of angels. What I was experiencing had more to do with who I was and what my soul purpose was. These sessions in heaven and angelic visitations were what I needed but not what everyone needs to fulfill their life purposes.

She also told me she had a few clients in the past that asked to be hypnotized for entertainment purposes, and if she felt someone wanted her help for any reason other than healing, she would decline them.

That evening I wanted so badly to share everything I had experienced in heaven with my husband while I was talking with him on the phone. I tried to open up to him, but after a brief minute of me talking, the conversation turned back to his day, the great meal he had enjoyed at his hotel, and his upcoming travels. I wish I could say that he was interested and listened intently to everything I wanted to share with him, but I think that for someone who is extremely logical, these topics were especially difficult to comprehend. After all, it was just *me* and he was not very interested in God, angels, or spirituality.

I longed for someone I could share these experiences with. Only Mabel had been witness to them, and she somehow seemed to journey with me and experience much of what I saw and felt. I longed to meet other people like me, as I knew they must exist. I am still hoping and yearning for this.

Mabel and I in Shanghai

CHAPTER

11

Our Soul Is Eternal

I n this lesson I once again was in heaven, and I was shown by a group of three angels in several different ways how my soul is eternal. I realize that these first examples are possibly classic ways of describing eternity, so they may not seem profound. It is not possible for me to describe how moving it was to experience this with the angels, who showed me incredible and beautiful picturesque images as they were explaining all of this to me.

They first showed me a beach and demonstrated how the life I was living now was really just like one grain of sand on a never-ending beach of what represented eternity. They then showed me the ocean beyond the beach and said, "Or you could compare it to one drop of water in a vast boundless ocean." The angels also said that the life I was now living was literally like "the blink of an eye" compared to all eternity.

They then explained to me how all of these traumas and the illness, although they were difficult at the time, did not really matter in the big scheme of things. These traumas provided excellent opportunities to learn lessons that I might not otherwise have learned. They provided my soul with the gift of the possibility for growth. My spirit and soul are eternal, and they will never die. And each difficulty made me stronger. The truth was that my soul remained whole, healed, and complete at all times.

They then showed me the most spectacular tapestry I had ever seen. The angels said that it represented my soul and its eternal life. It looked to be about twenty feet tall, and it appeared to have no end. They pointed out to me all of the various colors winding through and said that each color represented the many different people weaving in and out of my life. The colors were mostly very vibrant and meshed together absolutely perfectly. Even though there was also some black woven amidst the vibrant colors, this too added beauty and depth. They showed me a few small slits in the fabric, representing the major traumas I had endured. They said, "Do you see how insignificant these small slits are in comparison to this never-ending exquisite tapestry? When you see how your soul goes on forever, do you even notice those few small slits in the fabric when you look at it from our point of view?" When I saw things from heaven's perspective, these small tears did not matter at all. My soul acknowledged this. They again showed me that when I was in heaven before I came to earth for this lifetime, I knew I would have these difficulties because I had chosen them.

I was shown that any suffering I had experienced was all being used for something good and was all for my highest good. They told me that all suffering and literally every teardrop was saved and transmuted into something great and useful. I saw how Jesus really had gathered every one of my teardrops and was holding them in a container. Nothing was ever wasted.

There was one additional part that is still especially difficult for me to comprehend. It had to do with the angels being able to experience things and feelings with me as a human, which led them to be able to assist humans better while on the earth. This was also part of a sacred contract.

Once again after this session I was awestruck by the beauty of what the angels had just shown me. I was filled with wonder after I saw the beautiful beach, ocean, and the tapestry. I realized that there was a much greater order and a bigger plan for everything in the universe than I could have ever contemplated. I also took great comfort in knowing that every teardrop and every negative situation really is stored and transmuted into something good. None of our pain or sorrow is wasted.

Why Don't We Just Stay in Heaven?

In this lesson I was receiving hypnotherapy and was again together with three angels. This lesson was all about why we come to the earth instead of staying in heaven. This was possibly because at this time I was wondering why we didn't just stay in heaven or why one giant angel didn't come down and reveal all of this information to everyone at the same time so we all knew these truths.

I was told that it is a tremendous privilege to come to the earth for the opportunity of learning lessons and for the expansion and evolution of our souls. I was shown a line that consisted of thousands of people, all wanting to return to earth for this opportunity to grow and expand. It is also the journey of trusting in God and the divine within us without seeing everything in advance that causes expansion. It is during our most difficult times and trials that we learn the most important lessons regarding forgiveness, trust, perseverance, and patience.

The angels explained to me how in heaven there is only love, joy, peace, hope, and all related positive emotions. These are all of the highest vibrating emotions and the only ones in truth. Love is the highest vibrating emotion of all.

On the earth, because man has free will, we also have the opportunity to experience all of the contrasting or opposite emotions, such as fear, hate, despair, sadness, etc. These are all of the lowest vibrating emotions, fear being the lowest.

At any given time we have either chosen with our thoughts and actions to move toward love or toward fear. I am responsible to choose. No one can choose for me. Of course the more I move toward love, the happier I will be. It is not possible to continually choose fear and be happy. I was shown how I am much more responsible for my life than I previously had thought because I could decide which types of thoughts I would think, what I would say, and what my actions would be.

I was told that in heaven we still continue to learn and evolve, but it is not possible to experience hate or fear in heaven. I then saw myself in heaven. I was sitting in a classroom at a desk, and I was trying to learn about fear or sickness from a textbook; however, it was not possible. Although the teacher was excellent in her attempt to explain it, one has to experience it to understand it.

We choose to come to the earth for growth, expansion, and evolution. And it was in my most difficult times when I experienced the greatest amount of fear and grief that my soul evolved, was stretched, and expanded in the greatest degree.

It was explained to me that in this lifetime I also wanted to experience love on all levels and all extremes during my time on the earth. When I have experienced the extreme polar opposite of love on the earth, which is fear, it deepened my understanding of the highest form of love in the universe, the unconditional love of God.

I was told that I chose this extreme life for maximum growth and expansion of my soul so that I could have the greatest potential for reaching my soul purpose in this lifetime. It was a tremendous opportunity.

I was shown how before I was given the privilege of returning to the earth, I already knew that I possessed the strength to survive. And even if I did not and I passed away in this lifetime, it did not really matter in the big scheme of things, as I would return back to my home in heaven and eventually return to earth again for more learning and evolving opportunities.

It was demonstrated to me that we all come to the earth with our own individual curriculum. It is similar to attending school or college. We each have specific lessons we want to learn in varying degrees. Our guardian angels and spirit guides are similar to guidance counselors who help us to choose the right courses, arrange for us to attend the classes we need, and help us to find the most appropriate and willing teachers so that we can graduate on time.

The angels explained how everything was already planned ahead of time as far as people and teachers coming into my life. We chose to incarnate together. Sometimes the greatest teachers were the same people who caused me the most emotional hurt or harm in my lifetime. This provided me with important lessons on forgiveness, trust, perseverance, and patience. Ultimately in my case it also forced self-acceptance and self-love and reliance on God, Jesus, saints, and angels.

I was asked to be as nonjudgmental as possible of those who may be on a different soul level than I was. As I may encounter someone who appears to be in kindergarten on a soul level while another may be finishing what is equivalent of a master's degree, I was asked to be as tolerant, neutral, and non-judgmental as possible. This is very important as I observe others on their paths. I was shown that although my soul may be evolved in one particular area, another soul might be more evolved in a different area that is not apparent to me right away. They may be masters in one area, and I may be an amateur in the same area and vice versa.

Once again after this session I needed at least thirty minutes until I gained full consciousness. I was given so much information in this visit to heaven that I needed some time to comprehend all of it. Once again Mabel made the comment that I had just learned more during the two-hour healing session with the angels in heaven than I could learn from a thousand books. The first times she said this, I felt that she was exaggerating. But this time I knew that she was right.

Every time I was in heaven, there was not a doubt in my mind that the information revealed to me was the truth, and it was as though this truth was now etched into my heart and mind forever. However, as a limited human being, I still needed time to absorb and accept all of these new concepts. Ten years ago when I was being taught these lessons in heaven, all of these ideas and concepts were completely new to me.

The Monumental Museum

This time when I arrived in heaven, I was standing in the middle of what looked like a large university campus. The sidewalks and grass were immaculate. The grass was a vivid green, and it looked like there was a small diamond on the end of every blade of grass simply to make it more beautiful.

I saw small groups of people walking together and carrying books. They were wearing robes and looked to be around twenty or twenty-five years old. Everyone looked very happy like they were having fun! I knew each small group was studying or majoring in the same subject because their robes and books were color coordinated. This was possibly just for the purpose of me understanding this that day.

As I observed them together with the angels, they told me that learning in heaven is never dull and it is always fascinating, joyful, and exciting. What we study suits our interests and likes perfectly, and it is never boring.

I then noticed a monumental building made out of light caramel-colored marble about one hundred feet in front of me and to the left. The height and size of it reminded me of the museums I had seen in Chicago or Berlin, and it was possibly even larger. The shape of it was rather simple, as it was rectangular with a rounded roof. It was majestic-looking because of its size and the beauty and color of the marble stone. A portion of the exterior of the building was decorated with beautiful green vines. I did not walk to the building but rather thought, *I wonder what's inside of there?* And all of a sudden I was in the building.

A guide in the form of an angel greeted me. She was lovely and very kind. She acted much like a gentle, professional tour guide if I were visiting a nice museum on the earth. This building was a museum and a library. It was absolutely incredible and completely fascinating. The first floor was full of all of the most important original books and writings since the beginning of mankind on the earth. There were stacks of books in all different sizes, colors, and widths. Several of the books were very big, and others were very thick and old. Some were ornately decorated or had interesting seals, locks, or symbols. All of them were in the perfect original condition, even if they were hundreds of years old. The second floor was full of all of the most important historical artifacts from the entire world since the beginning of mankind on the earth. There were tables full of scrolls, stacks of more large books, carvings, inventions, paintings, and sculptures. There was a set of ancient tablets that I feel certain she said were the original Ten Commandments. There were many tables full of wonderful and amazing things to see. Everything was wonderfully organized and preserved. It was made clear by the guide that all of the things found in this museum were the original creations and the ones on the earth were replicas. The angel also pointed out that all of these incredible man-made inventions, writings, and works of art were inspired by heaven.

There were ladders used for traveling between the first and second stories. I was amazed by my agility in advancing up and down these ladders. My body was limitless, and I climbed up and down with great ease as if I was floating or flying. It seemed that whatever I could imagine, I could do. There were many people using these ladders and going up and down between the various levels in this museum, but I wondered exactly what the purpose was, as most of us were floating or flying, as if the ladders were just symbols.

There were many other people looking around the museum as well, but it did not feel crowded. Everyone was excited to be there, and every single thing was captivating. I thought, *Wow, my brother Bob would love this place!* All of a sudden he and some of my other brothers and sisters were there with me. We were in our prime age, and we were all thrilled to look around.

There was a beautiful stone staircase that led to the levels underground. This stone did not look like marble, but rather sand stone. Here, one level underground, I saw a large room with rows and rows of books, records, and files. It was like an immaculate white library. I am not sure what they consisted of, but I knew that they were significant. I had a feeling that this was where the sacred contracts were kept and I knew that it was not my place to go into this room. I did not hear anyone refer to them and I did not see anyone in this place.

I was then quickly distracted and fascinated by the incredible view outside the big open window in the staircase on what would normally be one level below the ground level. The view outside of this window in the staircase leading underground was a constant sunset below the earth. This sunset filled almost the entire horizon and it was the most spectacular sunset I have ever seen with many different incredibly vibrant colors. There were colors I had never seen before, which are difficult to describe. This constant view of the sun setting was there simply for beauty and enjoyment. There were possibly ten or twelve other people sitting and standing near me. We sat in this big open window, just enjoying the splendor. It was so breathtakingly beautiful and there was such an overwhelming sense of peace and awe that I did not want to leave. There was no glass in the window. It was a large rectangle, about eight feet high by twelve feet wide, which was almost the height and width of the entire wall carved out of the natural stone. It was somewhat irregular, as if it had been carved by nature. The opening was wide enough that myself and others could sit and enjoy this sunset. The stone was not hard to sit on but comfortable. Otherwise I never saw the sun in heaven as I think God was always enough to light up everything all the time.

There was also a very large beautiful garden with many lovely flowers of various colors outside and below the open window where we were enjoying the mesmerizing sunset. The garden looked as though it stretched to the horizon and proceeded as far as I could see on all sides. It did not look like a garden planted by man, but one by nature, like one of my favorite scenes in a French impressionists painting.

One thing comes to mind when I am thinking of how I can possibly describe how vibrant and alive the colors are in heaven compared to those on the earth, and it's the movie *The Wizard of Oz*. The movie begins in black-and-white while they are in Kansas, and then when they arrive in Oz, it turns into bursting, vibrant Technicolor. It is similar to that.

In heaven there consistently seemed to be anything and everything that one could imagine that brings enjoyment. It was as though I just had to think of something, and either I was transported to that place or it appeared before me.

The Majestic White Room

This is a vision I had while I was in a deep meditation with Mabel and her mentor and teacher, Paul, who was visiting from Vancouver, Canada. Mabel wanted Paul to meet me and asked if we could all meditate together. They came to our apartment in Shanghai. I hadn't expected to see or experience anything so incredible. Although this occurred in meditation, it was just as real as anything I had experienced while on the earth.

This vision began with what looked like a thousand tiny, dazzling bright white sparklers that gathered together to form the figure of a large male angel who was floating about twelve feet in the air. He had very large wings, was muscular, and was dressed like a warrior. It was the most brilliant bright white light I have ever seen. The light was somehow pleasing to my eyes despite the brightness.

The masculine-looking angel was holding the reigns of a brilliant white horse that was below and in front of him. The horse was pulling a large white square altar. In each corner of the altar was a wooden beam that supported a delicate roof. There were lovely intricate roses carved in the beams of wood. Standing in the middle of this horse-drawn altar was the blessed Mother, Mary. She was dressed in a radiant white gown and was wearing an exquisite crown. Her arms were open and slightly outstretched on both sides. It was a celebration for her, and all of heaven was showering her with affection and adoration. I knew that everyone in this glorious place was praising and adoring her. I could not only hear them, but I could feel them. The feelings were ones of pure love, genuine adoration, and the highest respect. However, it was not somber. It was joyful!

Then I saw that we were in a grand room. The size was larger than any theater or regal opera house I had ever been in. Beyond Mary, I saw a majestic open altar. It looked as though it was made out of white marble. God was standing in the center of it, and Jesus was standing next to him. I could not see the Holy Spirit, but felt that he was also present. In this vision I saw God, and he was an older man with a white beard, an image similar to in Michelangelo's famous fresco depiction of him in the Sistine Chapel. Although God appeared to be an old man, he was not frail or weak in anyway but very fit and lively with a playful twinkle in his eye! Jesus looked the same as I had seen him before. I was certain they both looked toward me and smiled just to acknowledge me, as if they were waving with their eyes and saying, *we see you!* I think every soul in that place felt acknowledged in this way. I felt as if I had won a rare prize of entrance into this divine event. Slightly beyond and above them was row upon row upon row of angels all adoring Mary. The angels went as far up as I could see. I knew that there was no end to this tower of angels all adoring the blessed Mother, the queen of all the angels. I could feel that all of the angels that formed this infinite tower were singing songs of praise but I could not hear them, I could only feel them. The entire room and everything in it was white but bearable for my eyes.

I knew that I was seated together with many other souls at this event. I did not see my body or the bodies of others during this vision. I felt as though only our souls were in attendance. It seemed as though we were seated on invisible bleachers. If this were the case, then I was in the middle of the right section about ten rows back and twenty feet high, looking down onto all that was occurring in this wonderful place. I could see everything perfectly. It was as though every soul in this room was united with the most- high King of heaven, his Son, the Holy Spirit, and the Queen of heaven.

This vision was life-changing. Although I already had a strong affection for Mary, after this experience it was heightened. While I was growing up, I was taught that Mary was the queen of the angels and of heaven and earth. However, this profound experience left no doubt in my mind that she really was the true queen of the angels and of heaven and earth. I was completely enamored by her presence. Her entire being radiated pure motherly love, strength, peace, hope, and joy.

I felt wholly honored to be given this glimpse of God and Jesus together on this magnificent white altar and to feel the overwhelming amount of love, joy, and adoration present in this place. I knew that it was a gift and that I was supposed to see this and now write about it. I was very fortunate to have visions of Mary and Jesus several more times in the following years. This was the only time I saw God in the form of a man and not as a white cloud of energy or glory.

I can not exactly describe what impressed me the most throughout this experience, but I must try. It was the feeling we each had of being unified with the Father, Jesus, the Holy Spirit, and Mary. We were willingly and genuinely adoring them as our true father, mother, and brother. It was not the type of *forced* adoration that we see Kings, Queens, and Princes receiving on the earth. In addition, it was feeling that we belonged to each other, similar to a closely unified family where everyone is unconditionally loved and accepted as they are. All souls were equally loved as God's children and heirs to the throne. Because of these things the joy was overwhelming and this was why we were all celebrating!

The Spectacular City

I visited many times a spectacular city in heaven. I was taken there in hypnotherapy, meditation, and very often in my dreams in the years between 2004 and 2009. It is the kind of dream where you are not sure if it was real or not when you wake up. Every time I was there, it was like watching an incredible high-definition movie of the most breathtaking landscape and places of worship I have ever seen, except I was *in* the movie. Again there simply are no words to describe what I saw and felt there.

The first time I was there, I was riding in what seemed like a small tour bus with four other people I did not know. There was a driver and an angel who was our guide at the front of the bus. I do not know why this time I was riding in a vehicle, as every other time I was in heaven I was walking or floating slightly above the ground. Or I just had to think about where I wanted to go, and I was there instantaneously.

In the bus the four of us were looking around in amazement. We were all pointing at the stunning scenery and asking one another, "Did you see that? Look at that!" I wished that the bus would go slower so that I had more time to look at everything. There was a beautiful blue river to our right that flowed along the road and into the distance. Rising out of the middle of the river were the most incredible and unusual mountains. They were not like any mountains I had ever seen before. Possibly the most striking mountains I have seen on the earth are the Dolomite Mountains in Italy, and these were far more impressive, as the stone was a beautiful golden color and not gray. They also were not jagged in nature, but more rounded, smooth, and flat on the top. I have only seen scenes of New Zealand in movies, but I wonder if its landscape is slightly comparable. The rich green color of the trees and vegetation were unlike any green I had ever seen on the earth. Every single thing about this bus ride, the landscape, and the city I was about to see was completely magical. Everything I experienced and saw in heaven was so far beyond anything I could have ever thought of on my own, as it was similar, but unlike anything I had ever seen before.

It is impossible for me to describe how marvelous, impressive, and spectacular every site was. When we came around a bend, we all gasped in amazement at the first glimpse of a city. From a distance it looked like it was made out of some kind of bright marble or stone and enhanced with diamonds or crystal so that it was shining very brightly.

Honestly the closest building I have seen on the earth that resembled those buildings glimmering in the distance is the tower portion of the Crystal Cathedral in Garden Grove, California, the church of Robert Schuller. However, it appeared to be five or more very tall towers in varying heights all nestled together with more buildings surrounding the towers. These crystal or diamond towers made the whole city gleam from a distance.

I was in several buildings that were larger than the size of the largest cathedrals I had ever visited in Europe. What I distinctly remember is seeing many beautiful different colored jewels in patterns on the walls and ceilings. I knew many of them were places of worship. One of these large places of worship was pure white and had a very large altar and was dedicated to God the Father. Another one was dedicated to Jesus and another to the Holy Spirit. The three of these circular places of worship were partially joined together into one but were three distinct buildings with three separate steeples. They did not look like man-made square steeples because they were very tall and round, gradually getting smaller in diameter as they ascended. I was somehow shown these three round buildings from above and it looked like three circles slightly overlapping one another. Every one of these buildings did not look like they were man-made, but rather perfectly carved out of one large amethyst or other crystal.

I remember seeing walls and ceilings that had many crystals and jewels of different colors. And one had an entire silver ceiling of what looked like the inside of an extremely large amethyst. The silver was a mix of many shades of silver and white. I was also in one that I knew was specifically in honor of the holy Mother, Mary. There were several different very large rooms in that one and many pearls used to decorate it.

Slightly down a hill from this cluster of buildings was an immense building that was again circular in shape and seemed to be divided into two or three different themes. This building was partially built into the earth as it was on a hill. The portion that was above ground had several very large rounded openings where one could enter. One of the sections of this enormous building was full of religious artifacts, possibly belonging to the saints while they were on the earth. This was the portion that was built into the earth. There was also one with many stone benches that resembled a natural amphitheater. While I was inside and looking around in this one, it seemed to keep expanding and be ceaseless. When I think of these places, I still am overcome with a feeling that I can not describe in words. It is possibly the feeling I would have if I were in my favorite most inspiring place on the earth amplified by a million.

There were golden sidewalks or pathways everywhere that connected all of the buildings in this city. The gold I saw looked like raw gold and was not shiny. Every time I was in heaven, the pathways looked the same, no matter where I was. It did not matter that the sidewalks were made out of gold and that there was an abundance of everything prized and precious in this place. There was not a lack of anything in heaven that we consider to be treasure on the earth. One time I saw what looked like the most beautiful big red roses I had ever seen growing out of marble or stone. Therefore, I can barely begin to describe any of these buildings, as they defied so many of the laws of nature on the earth and were unlike anything I had ever seen before because of their immense beauty and wonderment. I can still see them in my mind, and I wish my sketching skills were better or that I could somehow recreate them. There was a feeling of tremendous power and yet complete acceptance in all of these places.

Every time I was there, I was extremely happy to have returned again, and I felt an incredible sense of awe and privilege. I am not sure how many times I was there during the years between 2004 and 2009. I felt that every time my soul traveled there, it was a gift I was given that helped strengthen and renew my spirit. And every time I was there, it seemed like the first time, as I discovered more new things. However, I consistently felt like it was very familiar and that I was home.

Completely Missing the Point!

The following describes one other time when I was seated together with God. I feel that what God said to me at the end of this review was profound and life-changing. Of all of the messages and teaching I received in heaven, this is one of my favorites because of what God said to me.

This visitation to heaven began with me being escorted by angels to a white room. It was a review and assessment of several of my past lives, and they each had an underlying theme that I was carrying throughout this lifetime as well. God and the angels were asking me to finally break this cycle and to let go of my limiting beliefs and adopt a more truthful belief system, one that was aligned with God's truth about me. Some of these limiting beliefs were handed down from generation to generation. Others were developed in my childhood or even in past lives. These limiting beliefs and fears were keeping me from reaching my true soul purpose and even often caused my premature deaths in past lives. I love what God said to me at the end, and I have needed to remind myself often, as truly changing these beliefs did not come easily to me because they had very deep roots.

In the first life that I reviewed, I was a Carmelite nun in France. It was a beautiful fall day, and all of us sisters were gathering apples, pears, and walnuts from the trees and the ground and placing them into brown woven baskets. The atmosphere was very peaceful and joyful. We were all dressed in our work gowns, which looked to be made out of sand-colored burlap. I was walking with my sister (who is my sister Judy in this life) two by two in a line of around twenty-four nuns. We were the last in line. I looked like I was around seventeen, and she seemed nineteen. We were happily talking and singing. She had exactly the same beautiful singing voice that she has now. All of a sudden we were attacked by a group of soldiers on horses who wanted our large monastery and the gardens for their own. I watched as we were all killed. In this case it was my superiors who had been given warnings but did not protect us.

In another life I was the daughter of a wealthy and powerful man. Perfection was expected. Image was everything. To the outside world my father appeared good-natured, jolly, loyal, and safe. On our inside world there were many rules and little freedom. Although my father appeared to love my mother, brother, sisters, and I, he did not in any way seem to recognize our needs or feelings. He did many immoral things that hurt us. As his power and position grew, so did his ego. The bigger his ego grew, the more things he did to disrespect, dishonor, and disgrace us. His temper became more violent. As long as we obeyed the rules and did as we were told and did not complain about how he was hurting us, our needs would be met, and we would be treated well. If we disobeyed or disagreed, we were cruelly punished. Even though I was living a life of privilege, I felt as though I was imprisoned. All of my personal power and joy were slowly stripped from me. I observed all of us as we were seated in a richly decorated room filled with golden mirrors, all dressed in eloquent gold and white. We were waiting silently in this room together before making a public appearance. To the outside world we appeared to be very fortunate. On the inside we felt miserable and trapped. It was as if we were in a prison made of gold, screaming on the inside, but no one could hear us.

In this past life I was in Europe, and I believe it was during the Middle Ages. There was a very high city wall, and there were many starving people begging for food outside and below the wall. Sometimes people within the city wall would throw down scraps of food and vegetable peelings for the starving people below. The scraps were similar to those that might be given to a pig in former times. I was living in the countryside, and I had enough grain. I baked several round loaves of brown bread and brought them to the hungry people, which were a few miles away from where I was living. As I was about to reach them, I was run over by fast-moving horses pulling a wagon and was seriously injured and from what I could tell, I died. It appeared as though the man steering the horses saw me and ran over me on purpose to make a political statement because they were starving the people on purpose.

In this next life I reviewed, I was the head servant of a large manor. I excelled at my job and was very obedient and could keep the very large affluent house in perfect order. My cooking and baking skills were excellent, and I was wonderful at preparing the home for entertaining guests. But I had very little life outside of this job. I dedicated my entire being to pleasing my master so that he could enjoy a very comfortable life. I felt obligated to give up my life for my master because this is what I was taught was the right thing to do.

I saw snippets of several more lives where I was often a nun, priest, or monk. Everything was about following the rules perfectly and serving the church, the government, or someone else in authority and about being obedient and responsible. I heard the words, "Rules, rules, rules!"

After a review of these lives I was once again together with God. He said, "Wow, you were really obedient! You were very disciplined and followed all of the rules perfectly. You sacrificed your own needs and denied your feelings in my name. You even sacrificed your life. You thought that you were doing all of this for me.

"My dear one, you completely missed the point! I never asked you to be perfect or to deny yourself or your feelings. I never asked you to be a sacrifice. I never asked you for any of these things.

"Your life on earth was a gift to be enjoyed. What I wanted was for you to be happy. What I wanted was for you to understand and remember who you were through me and to live your most authentic and joyful life possible through me!"

Then the angels explained further. They showed me that in many past lives, my life was often cut short or I was seriously injured while I was trying to help other people. Although being of service to others is a wonderful thing and very important, I was consistently putting everyone else's needs above my own and denying my feelings and needs completely even to the point of it causing my own death. This seemed quite extreme and unbelievable to me, so they continued to show me many more examples when this was the case. They asked me to find a better balance and then I could be of better service to others.

They demonstrated to me how there also needs to be a balance between giving and receiving and that it needs to flow in a circle. They told me that only when my needs are met and I have allowed myself to receive as well as to give, could I then be of the most service to others. They asked me to practice receiving so that I could be of better service to others and have more to give.

They told me that I often gave away my personal power to others. Sometimes this was necessary for survival in past lives. However, they showed me that in many former lives and in this life, I often trusted others who made promises to stand up for me when I should have kept my personal power and stood up for myself. They encouraged me to only remain in relationship with those who honored and respected me.

I have a strong desire to remain humble. Some of it came from within, and some of it was projected onto me. I thought that to be a good Christian meant that I needed to be humble and "turn the other cheek." They showed me many lives where I was a monk, nun, or priest and this belief was reinforced. The angels assured me that although Jesus was humble, he was in no way weak. He spoke his truth.

It was at this point that it was revealed to me that my soul so much wanted to be close to Jesus and understand the suffering that he took on for the whole world at the cross, that I chose suffering in many of my lifetimes. It was physical, spiritual, and mental torment. Although what I had endured was merely a miniscule fraction of what he endured, it was as much as my soul could bear. They asked me to stop doing this. It was not necessary and it served no purpose. His sacrifice was already perfect and complete. I saw that it was the part of me that was so often a nun in prior lives that was choosing this and thought that it was necessary to become closer to Christ. They assured me that we were already as close as we could possibly be. They encouraged me to rather love, honor, serve, and spend time in relationship with him to remain close with him.

They also shared with me that although it is good that I care about those I loved so much, if I consistently protected them and cleaned up their messes, I robbed them of their soul lessons and could either inhibit or delay their growth as a soul. So they encouraged me to only help those who ask me for my help and to stop cleaning up other people's messes. I should only help others if they physically asked me and if I take pleasure in doing so and not because I feel obligated.

They then showed me my true power in their eyes as a child of God. They told me that if I could see myself as they saw me, I would see that I was magnificent, bright white and twenty feet tall. They asked me to forever hold this image in my mind, especially when I was facing the darkness or when others close to me were trying to suppress or break my spirit. They told me that I had more power in the small end section of my pinky finger than this darkness working against me had in the entirety of their unified beings.

After this session it took me a while to accept all that the angels had said as the truth. I was shown more lives where I sacrificed my life for others. I was startled to see how many times I was killed or badly injured while I was trying to help others. I wondered how I had not seen these things before. These limiting beliefs had been programmed into me from the time I was very young and over many lifetimes. It was as though I had been blind.

I was told that I was not given this life on earth solely to be a sacrificial lamb for others. The perfect sacrifice is already complete with Jesus. I cannot add to this sacrifice, and I cannot take away from it. It is already perfect, whole, and complete.

Wow! I was utterly amazed by the beauty of the messages that God gave to me. I realized immediately that it was a tremendous gift, and it was presented with such love. As I believe that all of us are called to heal ourselves and help others to heal, I feel that what God said to me could apply to many or possibly all of us on the earth at this time.

God told me that I do not need to be perfect. I had thought the opposite my entire life. I did not think that I was perfect, but I thought that anything less was unacceptable. I spent more time focusing on the 5 percent where I felt I failed than on the 95 percent that was good. He asked me to stop beating myself up for the 5 percent.

He was asking me to choose happiness instead of sacrifice. I learned that in choosing happiness, I ultimately would reach my goal of finding and working in my life's mission much quicker. In fact, it is much more difficult and almost impossible to find and work in my mission if I am not first happy.

He gave me permission to choose and accept my authentic self! This was very liberating, although I was not able to fully do this until this point in my life, almost ten years later.

I have been working on letting go of these beliefs and adopting a more truthful belief system during the last ten years and feel I have made a lot of progress. It has been a process and hard work.

Initially I could not completely see or believe the truth in what God and the angels were saying and how these past lives pertained to me in my present life. It was as though these false beliefs were so deeply rooted in me that I was blinded. After I received more healing, it was as though I suddenly woke up. It all made sense, and the blinders were finally removed in 2012.

It was only several years later, around 2010, when I realized that the past lives they reviewed with me mirrored my present life about 100 percent. And every way they were asking me to change was not just a pleasant way to live a happy and long life. But for me, as exaggerated as it may sound the change was actually necessary for my survival in this lifetime.

Review of More Lives

I had the opportunity to review several more of my past lives for healing purposes as well throughout my sessions with Mabel. What was most surprising to me was that in each of these lives, there was at least one person who was in my present life. While in hypnotherapy, upon reaching this deep state where one is able to access the subconscious mind, Mabel often asked me to look around and see if I recognized anyone. She told me to look into their eyes, as they always remained the same throughout every lifetime and therefore truly were the windows to the soul.

I saw at least six lives I shared with my husband, Michael. I saw at least one lifetime with my sister, my closest friends, as well as my friends from my choir in Germany. I was very surprised just how many people I saw in my past lives that were present in my life now.

The Analogy of God and the Sun

This was a lesson taught to me by the angels while I was in heaven. This is how they asked me to start visualizing and using the light of God to heal.

They said, "God the Father is like the sun." The sun is the star at the center of the earth's planetary system. It holds the solar system together. It is immense, glorious, and bright! It travels millions of miles toward the earth, radiating energy and light. It provides warmth and life to everything it touches on the earth. It sustains all life. It does not discriminate. It shines on every living thing. It is constant, and it never changes. It brings multiple blessings to the earth, causing all life to be nourished, to flourish, and to grow.

God's children are like the rays of the sun. They are all extensions of him and are always connected to their source. Their true and highest selves can never be anything but 100 percent sun. Even if they are on the earth and it feels like they are millions of miles away from their source, they are in truth no less sun than the source that they came from because they remain 100 percent sun. They only have to *wake up* and *remember* who they are in truth while they are on the earth!

They said that even when the sun is hidden behind clouds of gray or storms arise, the sun is still always present behind the clouds. Sin and unforgiveness are like dark gray clouds blocking the light and blessings from reaching us. Choosing not to have a relationship with God is similar to being caught in a continuous thunderstorm without an umbrella or any sort of protection.

All of this made sense to me, and I could relate to this analogy, as when I was first learning to meditate and send healing energy to others, both Mabel and the angels asked me to imagine the light of God like the rays of the sun breaking through the clouds. This was easy, as every time I went to heaven, it initially looked and felt like I was rising toward the sun. They then asked me to imagine the sun (God) shining directly onto the person I was praying for or myself when I was in need of healing. They asked me to imagine the light of God, which is filled with almighty power, healing, and strength, washing away every bit of pain and negativity, and filling every cell of the person with the healing light of God. This is what I began to do. I practiced this twice daily, sometimes for hours. This is the same method I was taught to transmute negative energy back to positive.

Because of all of the times I journeyed to heaven and felt as though I was being carried straight up toward the sun, whenever I see the sun breaking through the clouds, I can not help but think of God and every loving word he said to me and every thing he taught me.

CHAPTER

18

Children and Pets Are in Heaven

I had this experience while I was in hypnotherapy. It was different than all of the other ones, but I believe it is also significant and worth mentioning. This was my very last experience with hypnotherapy and the last time I was in heaven during hypnotherapy.

In this visitation to heaven a stunningly beautiful woman in a long bright pink gown greeted me. Her gown was shimmering like diamonds. She looked like a Disney princess with long blond hair, big eyes, and butterfly wings. I had never seen any being with wings like this before in heaven. She said she was a special kind of healing angel. At the same time she made it known to me that we were very close and that she loved me very much. I knew that I loved her and knew her too, but could not remember how.

She told me that I could not go farther than where we were and asked me to sit down in the soft grass. There was a golden path that was next to where I was seated. It was not a shiny, polished gold, but it looked as it is found in nature. There was a lovely lake to my right. The water was the most beautiful blue color I had ever seen, and it appeared to be sparkling with brilliant tiny diamonds.

I felt complete peace, understanding, joy, and safety. I could see that the golden path led to what looked like a magical and happy place. I could not see into this place because there was a very large tree blocking my view. I could see above the tree that beyond it there was what looked like the top of a stately version of the Neuschwanstein Castle in Bavaria, Germany, which the Disney castle is modeled after.

There were several children running by, and they were laughing and playing. One of them had a red balloon, and another was running together with a dog that looked like a golden retriever. They all looked and sounded very happy, even the dog. I knew that the children saw me, as they smiled at me as they ran by.

She was holding a healing wand with a lot of golden glittering light emanating from it. The wand was about two feet long, and the ball on the end was about six inches in diameter. She took some time and held this wand over various parts of my body, explaining to me which body part she was healing and why. There were negative emotions stored throughout my body, and she was helping to remove them.

She handed me an exquisite antique mirror to look at my reflection. I was very surprised to see that I looked like her twin except with brown hair, brown eyes, and a matching blue gown. We were otherwise identical. I didn't entirely understand this. From what I understood, the purpose was to boost my self-esteem because of all of my self-doubt when the angels kept telling me that I was a healer.

As I sat comfortably in the grass by this lake, she told me many things about myself as if she had known me my whole life. She then mentioned many things about my deepest desires that I had never told to anyone. Some would refer to these things as their hearts' desires. Your hearts' desire may consist of what we would dream of doing with our lives if there were no limitations. She shared with me what she saw and what she believed I was capable of if I let go of all of my fear and limiting beliefs and put my trust completely in God. She asked me to stop being afraid to be who I was born to be. She asked me to embrace my authentic self and to stop fearing what others thought or their criticism. She again asked me to look into this captivating mirror as she told me these things, and I was able to watch myself becoming all that she had told me that I was capable of becoming.

I believe the purpose of this was to increase my faith, confidence, and belief in myself.

She asked me to leave all of the hurt, pain, and fear that I had experienced in recent years with her. All of these things served no purpose now, as long as I remembered the lessons I learned. She encouraged me to walk confidently forward into my new life, where beauty would be traded for ashes.

Jobs in Heaven

I have seen several times since 2004, many people performing various *jobs* in heaven. However, this did not feel like the hard work we are used to here on the earth. What I saw was that every person who was performing a task was joyful and celebratory, as they were doing something that they completely loved, enjoyed, and were very interested in. It was as though every person had his or her dream job. Every job in heaven provided more joy, fulfillment, and satisfaction than any profession on the earth.

A few times I saw people in lab coats who were working to advance medicine or science on the earth by then working through and influencing or inspiring people on the earth with the help of the individuals' angels and guides. They were in highly advanced laboratories and were wearing what looked like safety goggles.

Although much of what I was shown regarding this work in heaven was far beyond my ability to completely comprehend, I understood that the work they were doing was for the good of the entire universe and for all of mankind. I also saw that they were continually searching for individuals on the earth with whom they could work through. These people were in touch with their intuition and were open to listening to the Holy Spirit and the angels.

My Highest Self

B efore I met Mabel in 2004, I don't think I had ever heard the term *highest self.* I believe if I had continued to live in the United States, I possibly would have been more familiar with these terms and topics.

I had been living in foreign countries since 1991 with CNN and BBC as the only English TV channels. Amazon did not yet exist where I was living. I could read German well, but I did not enjoy reading books in German. When I returned to the United States once a year, the English books I would bring back were my most important purchases, and a bookstore was always on the top of my list of things to do while in America. In addition, sometimes we were fairly isolated.

Furthermore, DVDs in English I bought in the United States did not work on foreign DVD players, as all of the disks are country coded. So until around 2007, about the only opportunity I had to watch a movie in English was on the plane ride home or when I was visiting the United States. Usually there was so much to do and family and friends to visit that I often did not have time. Later the Internet became a big help, but the German government blocked many websites from the United States. So in many ways I felt like I was living the last twenty-two years of my life in a restricted bubble, spending the majority of my time caring for my husband and daughter, learning about new cultures and countries, and packing and unpacking boxes.

Mabel explained to me that my highest self was the part of me that remained near to God in heaven and remembered my true identity as a magnificent powerful child of God. This highest self also retained the knowledge of past lives and the important lessons learned. This self also knew what the lessons were that I was working on in my current life.

She told me that I could access the knowledge of the higher self through meditation. I did not really believe this until I started to meditate regularly. I initially meditated together with Mabel and thought that I only received incredible visions and valuable information because of her influence, but I soon learned that this was not the case. After I incorporated meditation into my life on a twice-daily basis as she recommended, it helped me immensely on my journey and became almost as necessary for me as breathing. I consistently connected with God, Jesus, the archangels, and my angels in this way, and I honestly do not think I would have survived the last nine years without this connection.

When I was first shown my highest self, she looked just like I did when I was fifteen years old. She was wearing a simple, long white gown. At the beginning of this time with Mabel, I often saw her at the bottom of a steep staircase of about twenty stairs that were uneven in height. She was having trouble walking up the stairs and kept tripping and falling down. I understood the significance of the staircase. Each step represented a stage of growth or a major obstacle. Throughout the last nine years I saw her mounting step after step until she was near to the top of the staircase.

I knew that her name was Katherine. This was not very surprising to me, as my name, Karen, is derived from Katherine. I first remember having an affinity to this name when I was in the third grade and had to choose my confirmation name. We were asked to spend time thinking about which name we wanted to choose as our names, and I chose this one. I took great interest in reading about the different saints with this name. I was later able to visit some of these saints' birthplaces while I was living in Europe, such as St. Catherine of Siena, Italy, and St. Catherine Laboure from France.

Letting Go of
Limiting Beliefs

I n this session I was in in heaven to receive teachings about letting go of limiting beliefs. Throughout this session all of these lessons were demonstrated to me as well as engrained in my memory and heart. Limiting beliefs are beliefs that we hold either consciously or subconsciously that do not serve us in a positive way. They often act as obstacles to manifesting or attracting what we truly desire in our lives.

A limiting belief is usually passed on to us by those closest to us in our childhood and youth. They can also be influenced by or reinforced in adulthood by someone we perceive as having power or authority over us. Some can be handed down from previous generations. Beliefs are formed through repeated thought, and the only reason they have significance is because we've agreed that they are true, even if only a subconscious level.

I was shown that I had acquired many of these, and the angels asked me to try to release them so I could become all that God and my soul wanted me to be. If I were able to release them, I would have the highest potential of accomplishing my divine life's mission or soul purpose in this lifetime. I do not feel that these subconscious beliefs affected me as much when I was younger, but seemed to resurface and expand with the trauma I was experiencing as an adult.

One of these limiting beliefs was that I needed to sacrifice my needs and my happiness for the good of those around me. Another was that if I am not perfect, then I am not worthy of love or acceptance. The next involved my shame, believing I was not good enough because I was damaged. Lastly I felt I needed to remain very humble, and therefore, I often gave away my personal power because I thought it was wrong to shine my light in the world. I needed to learn to exercise my authority and be assertive in a gentle, loving, but firm way.

It was revealed to me how many of these limiting beliefs had been passed down from generation to generation on both sides of my family. It was shown to me, as if I were watching a movie, how they had been passed down to me from my mom, who had received them from her mom, etc. I then saw that if I do not work to replace my underlying belief system with a more positive, truthful system, then it was as though I would be handing all of these false beliefs on to my daughter. I was presented with a vision of her and I running a race and myself handing her a baton with all of these false beliefs on it. As I handed it to her, they were immediately transferred to her regardless of my intentions.

My soul recognized these limiting beliefs and really wanted to heal and release them so that I could be free of them. I also really wanted to let them go so that I did not pass them on to my daughter. One main reason I continued to go back for healing was so that my daughter did not have to struggle with what I had struggled with. I wanted her to be free of these things that had weighed me down in the most recent years of my lifetime. The angels often told me that the more healing I received and the more generational issues I managed to resolve, the more healing was passed on to Marie, and it ultimately would benefit all of those around me.

As I mentioned previously, I believe that I have made significant progress in the last years in letting go of these beliefs, but it has involved receiving help from healers and other professionals. I feel I am able to recognize thinking that does not serve me well much quicker than in the past and to change my thoughts accordingly. I am also much more vigilant in not allowing fear in. I am in no way perfect, but I have made steady progress.

CHAPTER

The Lost Souls

As I mentioned earlier, I would prefer not to mention anything about the lost souls, but I know I am supposed to deliver this information to those who have decided to read this book. It is possibly the most controversial portion of this book, but it also contains some of the most crucial information that I feel God wants me to share. Working in this realm with these souls was what God was referring to when he asked me to help his lost souls.

I understand that this may sound scary, unbelievable, and even crazy to write about this subject, but while I was working with these souls, the souls themselves were not frightening. It was just like talking with normal people I would meet on the earth, and it was very natural and even intimate and beautiful, except they were partially or sometimes almost fully translucent. It was as if I met every person on a soul level without the masks or egos that we sometimes carry with us while on the earth. The only thing that made it scary was the idea I had in my mind that this should be extremely frightening because death remains mysterious for most people. These lessons from God and the angels in this realm unlocked much of the mystery about life and death for me, so it was not frightening anymore. I was able to see how our souls are really in a miraculous and continuous cycle of life, death, and rebirth. Our souls never die; they only evolve.

As I had a very difficult time completely understanding why God needed me to do this work, I asked him why he did not just wave his hand or snap his fingers so that all of these *lost* souls could be saved? I knew that he had the power to do this. Why did he need a simple human being like me to do this job? Again, these questions seemed to come directly from my heart or soul, and I did not make a conscious decision to ask them. He explained to me that although he would like to, because man had been given free will while on the earth, he could not just immediately rescue them all. There are many universal laws in place, and this would be interfering with man's free will. Even the angels could not freely enter this realm. This is similar to why God cannot spare all good men from everything that we consider to be *bad* while on the earth.

I believe that this realm may be what some people refer to as *purgatory,* but this term was never used. This realm was subjacent to the earth. It appeared to be an exact replica of the earth's surface but rests about one foot below the earth's surface and realm. It is denser than the earth, and therefore, the molecules move even slower. Whenever I was there everything was gray.

The first time I was shown this realm, I was together with God. Following this, angels escorted me many times to this realm in between heaven and earth and showed me numerous times the cycle of life and death. What I saw, felt, and experienced there was so far beyond my former beliefs and understanding that I was taken there over and over again until I fully comprehended what my mission was with these souls. It was imperative that I understood it well and got it right.

I received a great deal of instruction in heaven and had many lessons with Mabel and the angels teaching me how to do this work. As I mentioned earlier, when I was told that I needed to learn how to do this, I thought that this was far beyond anything I was capable of. However, the angels insisted that I had the ability to do this. They told me that they would be working with me. They said that my internal light had been upgraded while in heaven and that I now carried it with me as an important tool that I would use for this and other work. They said that I need not fear it or push it, but it would all happen in God's divine timing. I should listen for instructions and follow each step as it was given to me.

As I previously wrote, the first time I was taken to this place, God was with me. This place looked like an immense never ending cave with dark gray stones. Below was a murky black river and the back of the cave was also black. When we arrived, I immediately saw thousands of souls in this place. These were the souls of people who had died but had not gone directly to heaven for various reasons. I did not see these people as they were when they had died, but I saw them as they were when they were living, except that their appearance was not completely solid but slightly translucent. The level of translucency or denseness seemed to vary and change.

There seemed to be no barrier between us. If they spoke a different language on the earth, it did not matter, as we understood each other perfectly regardless. As with all of the beings I encountered in these other realms, all communication was telepathic. As soon as I would see them, I would know their name, where they were from, and how they died. Often I would also know what their major soul lesson was while they were on the earth during their last lifetime on the earth. Some of them had been stuck in this place for many years.

Suddenly I saw what looked like floodgates opening up and a sea of souls flowing toward us. I recognized many people from my hometown that had passed away while I was growing up. I had not thought about some of them for many years, but I remembered them dying years earlier. These were good people from good families! I was surprised and saddened. I wondered, *What are they doing here?* They believed in God and even loved God. Many of them prayed and went to church every Sunday. Now this became much more personal, and I felt great empathy for them.

I was then shown in many ways how they did not understand God's great love and mercy for them. For many of them it was as though it was not their fault that they were there, as they had never learned or been told about the God that I now knew.

After the arrival of this sea of souls, I was made aware of the many reasons why all of these souls were in this realm. Some of them had believed in an angry God who would quickly cast them into hell if they had fallen short of perfection. Many of these souls were afraid of being harshly judged by God and damned to hell for all eternity if they had not confessed even one sin. If this were the case, then we would all be damned, as we all fall short of the glory of God.

They did not understand the true message of the New Testament, the good news that Jesus has already paid the price for the whole world and sacrificed his life for them. They did not know the truth that when you genuinely confess your sins to God, they are forgiven forever and remembered no more. They had maybe never heard these words before but had more often heard messages of fear, anger, and condemnation.

Other reasons why these souls were there was that they were ashamed of sins they had committed and felt that they were unworthy of heaven. As they were not certain of their salvation when they died, they hesitated and did not go immediately to the light. Some had addictions while on the earth and were still bound to them. Others were bound to earthly possessions or homes that they did not want to leave. Some had been shown all of the ways they had sinned and fallen short of deserving heaven by Satan after they had passed away. They had been tricked out of their salvation and were now in this place.

These souls were not in pain or suffering, but this place could potentially be very dangerous, as Satan was roaming about in this realm and wanted to steal for eternity what God had created. What I witnessed many times was that there was a real battle for every soul in the spiritual realms. It was again made very clear to me that God is the only Creator in the entire universe. Anything that Satan possesses, he has stolen.

These souls were now stuck in this place. For many of them it was as though they were lost and confused and did not know where they were. It seemed the longer they were there, the more confused they became. Some did not even know that their physical bodies on the earth were now dead.

God's Profound Love for the Lost Souls

I experienced in a most profound way God's deep sadness for these souls and his yearning for these children to return to him and their true home in heaven. There was also a great sense of urgency! He loved these children the same as all the others. He created each and every one of these souls, truly knew them by heart, and loved them unconditionally. He had literally counted every hair on their head, called them each by name, and treasured every one of them the same. Each of them was originally wonderfully and fearfully made in his image.

God said to me, "So many of my children cannot comprehend my love for them. What kind of a Father would I be if I allowed my children to go into a harsh environment where they will be tempted and they will fail? Then I condemn them to death if they could not perform perfectly and throw them into a hot fire and allow them to suffer forever? This is how some of my children see me. Who would want a father like that? I am not *that* God. I am their Father in heaven who wants desperately to bless each of them with more goodness than they can possibly imagine."

It was revealed to me that for some of these souls, and many people living on the earth, it was very difficult to believe that they have a Father in heaven who loves them this much and is this merciful, as they never had a positive role model of a loving father while on the earth. This fact saddened God greatly.

I was shown that it was often their own limiting beliefs about God and themselves and their relationship with God that caused them to now be in this other realm. If they did not understand how much God loved them and how they were worthy of heaven when they were alive, when they die, they would be less likely to go to heaven. It was much easier for Satan to tempt them and trick them into not going to heaven if they did not remember who they were as his child, or know that God is loving and merciful. That is why it is so important for us to have our faith and our beliefs firmly established while we are alive.

This realm was where I spent from two to six hours a day for the next four years, depending on how many souls there were to bring to the light and back to heaven. Archangel Michael and his army of angels as well as many other angels continually assisted me. It would not have been possible for me to do this work on my own, and I understood this from the beginning.

Initially when these souls kept coming through during my sessions with Mabel, she asked them why they came to me, as she had never experienced this great a number of souls before by any one individual. They would always answer the same way. They said that they were attracted to my light and to my big heart. It was true that my heart was sometimes too big for my own good. From the time I can remember, I have wanted to help people, and these souls were saying that they could feel this. I have always wanted to take away other peoples' pain and carry it myself. I believe this is how I was born. The reason I am mentioning this is that I believe that every one of us is already born with everything we need to perform our life's mission on this earth. From what I understand, from the moment I agreed to help these souls before I was born, I was given the tools to do it. I needed to learn how to use these tools. Then I had to diligently and consistently practice using them. As I was reluctant, I felt I was forced to practice using these tools over several years, which built up my spiritual muscles. I was maybe more stubborn or slow than some, as for me it really did feel like a sink-or-swim situation. I felt that either I did as I was instructed by the angels, trusted God and the angels, and used the tools I was given to battle the darkness, or I would sink and possibly drown. It was the forced battle that made me aware of my strengths and gifts. Without the battle they might still be lying dorment.

Throughout the first two years I helped each soul individually. This work took over my life and my sleep. I was fortunate, as my husband had always earned a very good salary. And very sadly from the time we moved to China, we rarely saw him for the next five years. However, this allowed me to do this intense work, which involved a great deal of time in prayer, solitude, and meditation.

After the first two years I developed a system of grouping the souls into different categories according to their ages. This was much more efficient and equally pleasing to God. I asked the angels to help me put a spiritual boundary between these souls and myself to maintain a higher level of physical and mental energy for myself. From then on I heard what sounded like a typical doorbell in my right ear when souls needed my assistance. It was the most incredible and practical thing. I have not heard that doorbell ring since 2008, and I believe this portion of my soul's mission is now completed.

Since this time I have met several spiritual healers who occasionally do this type of work in their practices, but possibly do not speak openly about it. They are just normal people like me. I also have never spoken openly about this part of my life to anyone except Mabel and these other healers who recognized it upon working with me.

The Steps for Helping Souls to the Light

The information in the following paragraphs is one reason I hesitated so long before I wrote this book. Throughout all of my experiences in heaven and in this other realm, there was never any reference to religion. It was always about our relationship with God, our Father in heaven, and/or Jesus, his son. As Jesus has always been my number one, this was difficult for me to understand. Then I heard, "Do you believe that I love a child born in Africa who has never heard my name less than I love those who have been born to more privilege and have?" As I have previously shared, the God I encountered many times in heaven was much more inclusive than I had ever imagined and did not discriminate based on religion or anything else.

What was most important to God was that each of these souls accepted or acknowledged him as their heavenly Father and/or Jesus as his Son and their Savior. As God, Jesus, and the Holy Spirit are all separate and yet *one* and cannot be separated, if you accept the one true Father, you also accept his Son. If you accept Jesus, His Son, you accept the one true Father. I realize that this is a very short and simple explanation of what the trinity is. I believe this has been discussed and debated for centuries, and many books have been written on this subject alone. This is how it was concisely explained and shown to me. From my understanding God is not as complicated as we sometimes believe him to be, and most of what he has created is meant to remain simple.

The next step was that he asked them for a simple and sincere apology, such as, "God, I am sorry. Or, "Father, forgive me."

Before ascending to heaven, it was also important that each soul realized what their main soul lesson was that they came to the earth to learn in their most recent lifetime. Often this lesson came to me as soon as I met each soul. If neither the soul nor I could recognize what their main soul lesson was, the angels revealed it to us.

Following this, I encouraged them to go to heaven and to the light. Some of them needed a great deal of encouragement and persuasion. Others needed to feel as much of God's love and light as I could possibly muster. In some cases I had witnessed Mabel using her right middle finger to tap them in the center of their forehead slightly above their eyes. This really seemed to wake them up when needed to the truth of their divinity as a child of God. I did this when necessary as well. When they agreed, I was able to boost them upward by using the light and love of God. I waved my arms in big swooping motions just as Mabel had. Once they were boosted far enough up, the angels escorted each of them to heaven.

I believe I witnessed thousands of souls going to heaven. Every single soul was greeted by someone in heaven who loved them. There was always at least one person and usually a group of people to greet them. All of heaven rejoiced every time a soul entered heaven. Every single soul entering heaven was considered an equal victory!

Teenagers and Children in This Realm

What I have written here is not to instill fear in anyone that their child or loved one may be in this realm. I would like to invite you, if one of your loved ones passes away, to encourage his or her spirit to go to heaven immediately without hesitation or fear. I feel that the following is one of the more important messages I am supposed to include in this book.

There were also some teenagers and children in this realm. Usually this was understandably because they did not want to leave their parents, siblings, and friends. They usually saw how their parents and friends were grieving. I did not see any children in the gray cave with the black river where I was first shown these *lost* souls. However, there were children and teenagers in another realm between heaven and earth. Children's vibrations are naturally higher than many adults because they have more recently come directly from heaven to the earth. Because they witnessed their loved ones grieving their death and did not want to leave them, they hesitated too long before going to the light and heaven and got *stuck*. That is why I believe, as difficult as it is, when a child dies, it is very important to give that child's soul permission to leave and encourage him or her to go as quickly as possible to the light. As difficult as it is to let them go and as much as you will miss them in this lifetime, know that for them it will only seem like a few minutes or hours, as the time in heaven is so different, and then you will be reunited for all eternity. Every child I ever saw in heaven was together with loved ones who had already crossed over and was being well taken care of.

In saying that, I must also say that if my child was near death or had just died, I would stand on the Word of God and his promises and pray that my child's life would return to its body. I would speak scripture over my child out loud and would ask God, Jesus, and one hundred thousand angels to bring my child back to life and muster every ounce of faith that I have in believing that my child would return to life. I would ask for the prayers of every church member, family member, and organization that I could. However, if my child or loved one had clearly passed away for more than one day, I would immediately pray for my child's soul and ask God, Jesus, and the angels to escort her to heaven.

I have never seen any soul that wishes for the remaining family on the earth to be sad. It is normal and necessary to grieve, but if possible, as difficult as it may be, do not hold on to the soul of your loved one and hold it back. Let it ascend into heaven. Once they are in heaven, they are safe, and after a short time, they are usually by your side almost every time you think of them. I think most people would be surprised how often our loved ones come to check in on us or spend time with us. I did consistently witness how much the souls in heaven wish their loved ones on earth happiness and peace. I also witnessed many times that when parents died prematurely they stayed by their children's sides in spirit almost constantly and were with them throughout every event in their lives, including every trial and every triumph. Often the deceased parent wants the living child to know that they never left their side and were always with them. This was the same for children who died prematurely. Their soul remained by their parents' side almost continually, and did not miss one family event.

My purpose in writing the above section is not that you now worry that your loved ones are in this realm, but if they have passed away, encourage them to go to the light if they haven't already. And if your loved ones pass away, don't hold on to them in spirit. Pray for them and encourage them to go to heaven as soon as possible.

Special Healing Chambers

I saw a special place where a few souls went when they returned to heaven. These souls had undergone extremely traumatic illnesses or injury, suicide, or spiritual torment, or for other reasons they were in need of more intense healing. These souls were in special beds that looked like the most comfortable beds I have ever seen and were special adult-sized rocking beds. The angels were gently rocking these beds back and forth like a mother with a newborn baby. These souls were receiving constant love and healing from the angels. I once saw someone who looked as though they were in an adult sized incubator. There was not a doubt that these souls would again be made completely whole.

A Glimpse of Hell

Out of the thousands of souls that I have worked with together with Mabel and the angels, I only ever saw two souls that went to hell. One of them was very proud and he refused to accept God as his Father or Jesus as his Savior. And the other was a Satan worshipper, and he had his head tattooed to look like Satan. He made his own decision to go to hell as he preferred to be with Satan and refused to go to the light.

I believe there was one time I was shown a distant glimpse of hell. This was in a very vivid dream during the most intense time of angel visitations and journeying to heaven in 2004 and 2005. In this dream there were many people waiting to board a long train on top of a high rocky cliff. Most of the people were wearing coats, and some were carrying travel bags, as if they were on a journey. Some of the clothes they were wearing looked to be from prior years going back to the 1920's. In order to board the train, they had to step over a two-foot-wide crack or fault in the cliff. I could see that this crack was at least as long as the train was. The train was very long, and I could not see the end of it. Between the big crack in the rocks I could see far below the earth's surface a huge burning fire with leaping yellow and orange flames. I knew that this was hell. I was shown that I was to help the long line of people over this wide crack in the earth and into the train where it was safe. I needed to do this as quickly as possible. It was urgent! In this dream my daughter and I were working as a team, assisting the people into the train as quickly as possible and encouraging them and helping them over the fault with the burning fire below.

Energy, Frequency, and Vibration

B efore I began to work with the lost souls in this other realm, I was taken to heaven many times, and the angels gave me many lessons on energy, frequency, and vibration. It was explained to me that everything in the universe is composed of energy and therefore has a vibrational frequency. Science, through quantum physics, has verified that everything in our universe is composed of energy. Everything is vibrating at one speed or another, including us. The speed at which something is vibrating is called the frequency.

God is the highest vibrating being in the universe. The angels are vibrating at a very high frequency, and they have the ability to go between God and man, who are vibrating on a lower level. Although some humans on the earth have raised their vibration enough to connect with the celestial beings, this realm where these lost souls are is even denser than the earth, and therefore everything, including the souls there, are vibrating on a lower level than the earth. The vibration is so low that the angels cannot enter freely and help these souls. The reason why they needed another human being to work as a bridge between these two realms is because of the huge difference in the frequencies of their vibrations. As previously mentioned, neither God nor the angels can interfere with man's free will.

I was instructed on keeping my vibration high enough to do this work. The angels told me that the very best way to raise my vibration was through consistent prayer and meditation. Things that also help to maintain a higher vibration are keeping my thoughts and emotions positive and doing things that bring me joy, like singing, spending time in nature, laughing with family and friends, or watching funny movies. This is true for everyone. I was told that I could choose positive thoughts and resist negative ones and stay in Christ's peace. In a peaceful position I maintain my power. People will offend me, and life will happen; however, I choose how I will react and if I allow them to take my peace, thereby lowering my vibration and my personal power.

I am typically a happy and an optimistic person, which I believe has helped me throughout my lifetime. However, I am also someone who naturally has many thoughts running through my head at any given moment. When I was very ill before I met Mabel and learned to meditate, my mind was almost constantly racing with many of the thoughts being ones of worry. I was not even aware of this, as it had become normal for me. My mom worried a lot, and I possibly learned this behavior or inherited it. I have since heard that if you can worry, then you can meditate, as worrying is the negative form of meditation. Think of how powerful we could be if we turned every thought of worry into a positive thought of possibility. After I began meditating, my mind became still and much more quiet, and I have not experienced my mind racing with thoughts of worry for many years.

Everyone has the ability to communicate with angels and to hear God's voice. I am not unique in this way. From what I understand, we all have the same intuitive capabilities. It just needs to be consistently practiced. The best way to do this is to take some time every day to be still, quiet your mind, and listen. I was told that praying is when we talk to God and meditation is when we are still and listen. When learning to listen, it is important to discern where the information is coming from. The voice of God, your angels, and highest self will always be loving, consistent, and hope filled. Information that stems from darkness is fear based, inconsistent, and fills you with doubt.

Never underestimate the power of just one person in prayer. One person can make a tremendous difference in the universe. I was shown how prayer is amplified and multiplied when two or more people are gathered to pray. Most people have heard this from Matthew 18:19. However, the angels made this apparent to me. This phenomenon is even much more powerful than I had ever realized. This is the same when praising God with song. I have seen how heaven opens up and miracles are released when people are gathered together and praising God. When I was made aware of how powerful this is, I tried to begin my prayer and meditation time by thanking God and Jesus and praising them, even if it was only for a few minutes. I try to remember to praise them extra when I am in the middle of a storm or battle.

CHAPTER

My Shadow Side, Sin, and Forgiveness

Meeting the Tibetan Monks

I received many lessons about my shadow side, sin, and forgiveness while in a hypnotherapy session. It was on this day that I had the unique pleasure of meeting two of Mabel's Tibetan monk friends who were traveling through Shanghai on their way back to India. They were wearing the traditional maroon-colored robes with a bright yellow shirt underneath and were associated with the Dalai Lama.

As we were introduced, Mabel asked me to place my hands together over my heart and to bow my head. They greeted me with their traditional embrace by placing their forehead directly next to mine, and their hands on my shoulders. I had never felt anyone acknowledge my soul in this way. My soul rose up to greet them in a way I had never sensed before. I felt as though my soul itself was embraced and recognized their souls. I was especially surprised to feel this level of acceptance and recognition from two people I had never met before. It was again a situation where we did not speak the same language, and yet I knew we had communicated on a soul level and words weren't even necessary. The following are the lessons I learned after meeting them while in a hypnotherapy session.

My Shadow Side

I was told that everyone has a shadow or dark side. The angels very clearly showed me my dark and light sides. I saw them as a dark gray snake representing my dark side and a cream-colored snake representing my light side. These two snakes were tightly coiled around my spine, forming what looked very similar to the medical symbol or caduceus. The two snakes were equal in size. The angels asked them to come forward and out of my body so that I could observe them more closely. Then they uncoiled and were both lying directly adjacent to my spine. The cream snake was to the right, and the gray snake was to the left. They then became solid like two poles. The angels lifted them from my spine and held them close to me so I could look at them and hopefully stop fearing my shadow side as much as I did.

As I did not want any darkness at all to exist inside of me, the angels asked me to love and embrace my dark side equally to my light side. In loving it, I accept myself and do not fear the shadow side of me. As whatever we focus on expands, if I fear it and place my focus on it, I give strength to it. If I embrace it with the love of God, I strengthen my light side. However, embracing my dark side does not mean submitting to it.

I was told that as humans, we all have a shadow side, and we all will be tempted. I feel I understand temptation well, as I think I have been tempted about as much as most anyone. There were many times I needed every ounce of my strength to resist temptation. We each decide what we will do with the temptations. The angels told me that if I have strengthened my light side, then I could more easily resist future temptations. However, if I have yielded to the shadow or dark side in the past, then it grows in strength. This makes it more difficult to resist temptation when it presents itself again. Giving in to temptation is what we humans call sin.

If God's Mercy Is Infinite, Am I Free to Sin?

Because God bestows his infinite mercy to us does not mean that we are free to sin. There are always consequences for every thought and every action, as there are many universal laws in place. Therefore, there are many ways that sin affects us.

The angels instructed me that when I sin, upon recognizing it, confess it immediately to God. Accept his forgiveness. Forgive myself. And try my best to do better tomorrow.

Regarding sin, one of the most destructive roles that it plays in our lives is that it places a barrier between God and ourselves so that his blessings cannot reach us. It also causes our hearts to harden. When my heart is hardened, I am unable to receive the blessings of my divine destiny. The more I sin, the more layers or what look like hard shells of negative energy are placed around my heart.

Often we do not realize the consequences of our thoughts and actions and regard them as harmless. I once observed a person swearing and speaking negatively, and they were drawing a black mist to themselves with every negative and swear word that they spoke. This mist was fear, and it was going into their mouths. I have seen this as well when someone was reading a dark book or watching a dark movie. What is so detrimental is that this dark mist attracts more darkness or negativity. So with every thought and every action, we are constantly choosing to be either moving toward love or toward fear. Since this time I often think how many people are completely unaware of how they are damaging themselves by watching violence or reading dark-themed stories. Thoughts of fear attract more fear and the other negative vibrating emotions, while positive thoughts attract more love and the other higher-vibrating emotions.

In addition, just as prayer, meditation, positive thoughts, positive emotions, and joyful activities raise our vibrational frequency, sinful acts and thoughts have the opposite effect and lower our vibration. Although we may feel a thrill or short-lived excitement from sinful acts, it goes against the true nature of our being, so it is not true joy or power but counterfeit feelings that fuel the ego.

When our vibration is lowered, it makes it more difficult to hear the voice of God, the Holy Spirit, our angels, our spirit guides, and our own intuition.

I was informed that I would attract people and situations of like vibration to myself. I learned that what I focus my energy and thoughts on today would be what I experienced tomorrow.

The next way sin hurts us is that is creates guilt and shame, which can be difficult to release. It also often leads us away from our divine destiny and gives the Devil exactly what he needs to trick us or tempt us after we die.

Lastly, sin usually hurts other individuals we love, and this ultimately harms us. All of our thoughts and actions, whether positive or negative, will always return to us.

In recent years I saw someone very close to me often surrender to his shadow side. His sins became increasingly dark, and therefore he associated with people trapped in the same level of darkness. He was then caught in what resembled a monstrous sticky spiderweb. He was so entangled in darkness that he was unable to free himself. His heart became hardened, and layer upon layer of tough shells formed around his heart. He appeared to be blinded by sin and was miserable in every way. He lost everything and everyone he loved, but he could not see that it was his own actions that had caused him this tremendous pain. What it especially sad is that when you are once blinded in this way, it is very difficult to find your way back into the light and onto the path of love.

If you are doing things in the darkness, do not be fooled in anyway! Do not believe that these things are done in secret, as everything will always eventually be brought into the light. These things will affect you and spread like a fast paced cancer to your family and those closest to you. Again, dark activities attract negative energy and it attaches itself to us like glue and spreads to those closest to us.

For Every Action There Is an Equal Reaction

Furthermore, for every action there is a like and equal reaction. For every thought we think and everything we do, we will attract an equal force to us of equal frequency. So if we speak negatively about someone, those negative words will come back to us similar to a boomerang and harm us. And if our behavior hurts others, then this hurt will be returned to us. It may take some time and may even accumulate over time, but it will return to us. On the other hand, when we help someone or show kindness to another, this, too, will return to us. It may not return immediately, but it always will. This is a universal law.

In like manner, if we fill our day with thanking and praising God and dedicate everything we do in our day as a prayer or thanksgiving to God, we will be blessed in equal proportions. Almost everything we do in our day can be offered as a prayer to God. This does not even need to take long. It can be as simple as when we first wake up in the morning and say, "Thank you, God, for another day. I offer this day to you. Please guide me and show me what you'd like me to do today. How can I be of service to you or someone else today?"

What would please God the most would be that we would have such a strong relationship with him that we would choose not to sin because we knew that it does not honor him. His hope would be that we understand his love for us and desire a strong loving relationship with him. As with any relationship, the more time you spend with someone, the closer you become.

I feel that there is one thing God wants me to add here. There are many who understand all of the principles mentioned here very well. I believe that there are several excellent books written on these or similar subject matters. The authors teach them beautifully and with authority but refer to God as the "Universe" or "Universal Energy" or something similar, as if they are ashamed to say the name of God. He realizes that there are many who can not relate to a loving father as they have not had an example of one in their lives, and therefore can more easily relate to the term "Universe." However, he would prefer that no man be ashamed to call him God, Father, Papa, Daddy, or any name that is most familiar and affectionate for you—the more affectionate, the better. He would like to receive credit where credit is due. He is the one and only Father and Creator of the universe. He does not feel much appreciation or affection when he is called Universal Energy. This denies him affection and glory.

Lessons on Forgiveness

I was given many lessons on forgiveness. What I believe is that with God we are at any given time one short prayer away from forgiveness.

I was shown how holding on to unforgiveness in my heart is similar to drinking a small portion of poison every day and hoping that the person

I am angry at will get sick or suffer. It can be very difficult to forgive someone who has deeply hurt us. By forgiving them, I am not condoning or excusing what they have done, but I am freeing myself of this hurt and suffering. In these last years I have had more to forgive than I ever could have imagined. But I realize that I needed to do whatever I could to try to continually give any unforgiveness to heaven and the angels. I understand that holding onto this hurt will only make me ill and serves no positive purpose. The angels told me often that if I asked, they would help me to release it. I learned from one healer to imagine an angel coming with a bucket. I then put my hurt and anger into it. She or he then brings it away and it is transmuted back into the light. I then continually bless the person who has hurt me and has caused me grief. This initially feels like the most unnatural and difficult thing to do, but once I tried it, I learned that it is also the most effective. I learned that I felt more peaceful and stronger when I did this than I did when I kept rehearsing in my head how much they had hurt me. When I keep reliving the trauma, this causes me to feel stuck and powerless.

How we go about our daily lives regarding our connection to God will determine our eternal destiny. I experienced thousands of times, that each soul had a last chance to accept God and repent, even after their death. If they died fearing God and his judgment and avoided God and the light and Satan got to them first, they could be *lost* for all eternity. This is why we need to be very clear that we are his children while on the earth so that we will live for all eternity in heaven. This is not because God will not accept us back into the kingdom. It is because if we are not sure where we stand, then the Devil has a much better chance of tempting us with our own shame and guilt and showing us every way that we do not deserve heaven and talking us out of our salvation and leading us into this other realm. As I mentioned earlier, what I saw was a very real battle in the spirit world for every soul.

God Wants Us to Be Abundant in Every Way

It was revealed to me that God loves us so very much that he wants each of us to experience unlimited abundance while we are on the earth.

This means an abundance of love, happiness, health, wealth, joy, etc. This includes whatever your heart's desire is, as long as it is within God's will. This is our divine destiny as his child. I was shown how everything that is abundant is already waiting for us, similar to a huge warehouse of presents in heaven ready to be sent by express mail to us and opened. But our hearts need to remain soft and close to his. When we sin, we cut off this supply, and we receive the result of sinning, which is rotten fruit and the worst gifts that the universe has to offer. It may be that our actions take a while to catch up with us, but they always do.

I was shown how God does not want us to suffer and he is never the reason for our suffering. Only good things can transpire from God. He does, however, allow these universal laws to exist as well as the darkness on the earth for the purpose of our soul's expansion and evolution.

Mabel and her Tibetan monk friends in India

The Gifts I Received in Heaven

After my first journey to heaven in 2004, I could see and speak with people who are in heaven. There are times when it has been much clearer and stronger than others. It is not as clear now as it was the first years when it seemed there were no perimeters between us. Since then I have established much better boundaries so that I can live a relatively normal life. I have always felt that the angels have complete control over whether or not I communicate with someone who has crossed over and every time it has happened it has been divinely orchestrated. I have never sought this out. It began happening to me after my first angelic visitation and journey to heaven. I have delivered the messages when the information has helped an individual to heal and if the recipient is willing to receive the messages.

During these first years beginning in November of 2004, I was overwhelmed by many souls in heaven wanting me to give their loved ones on earth messages for them. Especially during the year that I was having healing sessions with Mabel, my spiritual vision and knowing were so clear that I often received the full names of the individuals they wanted to get a message to, where they lived, and sometimes even telephone numbers. Having the ability to see and speak with people who had crossed over initially felt like a nightmare to me. It took several years for me to see this as a blessing. I found it to be traumatic, and I did not view this as a gift, although Mabel told me that it was. Since that time I have repeatedly asked for much less information from those who have crossed over, as I found it is very difficult to live on the earth and be bombarded with constant information and feelings that belong to someone else. I still am working at establishing better boundaries.

The people from heaven themselves were not frightening. I saw them as beautiful and in the prime of their lives. However, it was the whole idea of it that disturbed me the most. I knew that I was not crazy. If I possibly had known just one other person like me, it may have helped me not to feel so strange and alone.

One thing that was evident to me was that once a person reached heaven, he or she was not immediately all-knowing. But from my understanding these people now had easier access to all of the knowledge they had accumulated in previous lives. Their personalities remained very similar to how they were on the earth minus much of the ego. They did have a much better understanding of many things, including how their actions had affected people that they loved while on the earth. Therefore, they often wanted to apologize to their loved ones for something they had done or had neglected to do. The other most common thing they asked for was for me to tell their loved ones that they were okay and that they loved them. And the third most common occurrence was parents wanting to express to children, often now adult children, how proud they were of them and that they were always with them throughout their entire life, through every trial and every triumph.

All of the people I have ever met in heaven always wish the people they love on the earth love and happiness. I heard numerous apologies and loving wishes from those in heaven toward their family members still on the earth. It is amazing to me how much healing can occur when someone says a heartfelt apology.

After several years I eventually got used to it and accepted it as a gift. I stopped fighting it. I saw the beauty and healing in what was occurring when people visited me in our home and received a loving message from their loved ones who had crossed over into heaven. I watched their faces and dispositions change as burdens were lifted from their hearts and minds and replaced with peace. I witnessed healings occur, as people were able to stop grieving their loss and realized how close their loved ones still were, even though they were now in a different realm.

It is only very recently, almost ten years later, that I can openly admit that I have this ability. This was not only because of the fear of people thinking I was crazy but also because of the Bible verses regarding consulting a medium and how it is wrong. Although I know with all my heart that I am called to do this work, I believe that with all gifts everything depends on your intentions and how one uses them. I believe there are those who use these gifts in darkness and those who use them in the light of God for healing purposes. I do not know if this is part of my future, as this is entirely up to God. I chose the following two stories of souls in heaven that affected me particularly positively. They are two of my favorite stories amongst many.

A Loving Couple from My Hometown

As previously mentioned, in the first few years after I was in heaven for the first time in 2004, many souls from heaven came to me asking for my help in delivering messages to their loved ones on earth. It was as though there was no barrier between us. I initially found this traumatizing and frightening. I resisted this for a long time. I did not want to deliver messages in any way. I did not want to admit to anyone that I could see and speak with people who had died, as this was far too weird. Then something happened with a loving couple from my hometown, and I had no choice. I feel this is a beautiful story, and to this day when I remember it, it helps me to accept and see this ability as a gift. I have omitted their names for anonymity.

One night in 2005 while meditating, a man came through to me. I saw him just as I knew him when I was younger, except he was partially translucent. At times when he was moving, he was more translucent with only the outline of his body showing. He desperately wanted to get a message to his wife. He said that he had died suddenly and he didn't have a chance to tell her good-bye. He loved her very much and wanted to tell her one last time how much he loved her and to be able to tell her good-bye.

He also shared a few personal messages. Most importantly he wanted to encourage her to go on with her life and enjoy the time she had left on the earth. He said she was grieving a lot and was having a very hard time enjoying her life without him.

I knew this couple and their children while I was growing up. I did not know them well, as they were not in our direct neighborhood and most of their children were older than I was. He was known for his love of horses and had several large draft horses in a field outside of my hometown. I drove past these marvelous horses occasionally.

I don't think I had seen or spoken with his wife since I left for Germany in 1991. I believe the last time I saw him was in 2000 when I was home for the parish fall festival and he was giving free horse-drawn wagon rides to the children. He had some of these strong workhorses pulling a large wagon lined with bales of hay for the children to sit on. Our daughter, Marie, enjoyed several rides on his large wagon.

I did not want to call her, and I did not want to deliver the messages. This meant that I would have to admit to someone in my hometown that I could see and speak with dead people. At this time only the healer and a few of my siblings knew. It did help that I had had the previous positive experience with my great-grandfather and my dad. But this was different, as this might possibly mean that others from my hometown would find out. I was also afraid of her thinking that I was out of my mind, as I wasn't sure if she knew me well enough to know that I wasn't.

He was very determined and persistent. He consistently tried convincing me and kept asking me to call her. Finally after he kept me awake most of the night, I agreed. He was then very happy and thanked me. I could see and hear that it was not only he who was persisting but also both of our angels.

The next morning I called Mabel and told her what had happened and asked her if she felt I should make the call. She told me that it was important that I did and that I should follow the angel's instructions and do it!

I first called my mom to ask if this man really had died. I was living in Shanghai at the time. Throughout all of the years since I had first moved away from home, first to Iowa State University at the age of eighteen, I called home every week. My mom had the habit of usually telling me who had recently died. I didn't remember hearing that he had passed away. She confirmed that he had passed away a few months before in March of 2005 and that he had died very suddenly.

Then I called his wife as he requested. She was surprisingly open. When I told her that he had come through to me and that he wanted her to know how much he loved her and that he was sorry he didn't get to say good-bye, she began to cry. She said that she had prayed every day since his death for a sign that he was okay and in heaven. She had watched for signs but was not certain if she had received any. She said that now her prayers were answered. I heard the joy and relief in her voice. I felt that she believed me and did not think that I was crazy.

We also talked about the importance of her going on with her life and trying to enjoy her life again. I felt as though the angels were speaking through me to her. By this time I had often seen how for our loved ones in heaven time is much different. I told her that although he loves and misses her dearly, he is not suffering and he doesn't need to wait every minute for her. I saw many times that the time in heaven is much different than it is on the earth. Although she may live twenty more years, it may only seem like an hour or a week for him that they are apart. What he truly wanted most of all was that she be happy and enjoy her life. I asked her to please not tell anyone about our conversation, as I was afraid of what people might think.

She said very matter-of- factly, "So you're a medium?"

I said, "I don't know. What exactly is that?"

She said, "It's someone who can speak with people who have crossed over."

I said hesitatingly, "Well, I guess I am." I was very surprised that a faith-filled woman of her golden age knew this term and was not fearful of it.

She then said, "I can tell it must have been difficult for you to make this call, but I am very thankful that you did." I felt she had a tremendous amount of fortitude and wisdom while I was speaking with her. I have often felt this when I have spoken with the strong women from my hometown parish. I was very grateful that she was so open, and I felt strengthened by her.

I then joked with her and asked her if her husband was persistent and determined while on the earth. I told her how he bugged me the entire night until I agreed to call her. She said, "Oh, yes! If he wanted something, he would pester and bug me until I would give in."

I thought, *Exactly!* We both laughed. At the same time I could see he was also laughing out loud and almost jumping up and down with joy, as he was so happy he got through and was rather proud of himself! To him, this meant a lot. He looked like he had won heaven's version of the lottery and was as surprised as I was that this was even possible. He had been searching for a way to get through to her, and I was it. Directly following this, I saw a symbol of a bridge in my mind and remembered that the angels had asked me to be this bridge.

When we hung up the phone, I felt relieved and grateful and like I had just done something worthwhile. I felt a huge sense of fulfillment and gratitude. I could again see him, and he was beaming and laughing and again, literally jumping for joy. Then almost immediately he had another request. He asked if I could call her back and ask her to tell the children how much he loved them and that he was sorry he didn't get to say good-bye. There were also some more individual private messages. I called her back and gave her these messages as well and asked if she could keep my name anonymous to their kids. Yes, and now I am putting this all in a book for the whole world to see what I had tried to keep secret for so long.

A short while after this I had a wonderful vision of him again. This time he was seated on a white rocking chair on the porch of a nice white ranch-style house. The porch was the big, open, old-fashioned kind. Seated next to him was his good friend, who is also from my hometown. They were looking at a big beautiful pasture with some rolling hills in the distance. In the pasture were five strong horses running free. The horses were galloping back and forth in unison. It appeared as though the long, brilliant green grass and colorful wild flowers were dancing with them as they were swaying back and forth in perfect unison. He and his friend were talking and reminiscing and admiring these magnificent creatures. This was the second time I had seen animals in heaven. It also gave me the impression that this was his idea of what heaven would be for him. He was completely joyful and content and had the company of his good friend.

This gave me yet another perspective of heaven and the knowledge that what we experience in heaven will be what brings us the most joy. It seemed to me that we have some ability to create in heaven what brings us the most happiness—of course, within God's will.

Months later when I was home and with my mom and dad, I asked my mom if this other man I saw with him sitting on the porch in heaven had passed away. My parents confirmed that he had, and my dad added that he was a good friend of the other man from my hometown. I had not even asked that question, but my dad provided an answer to the question that I especially wanted to ask before I could even ask it. I did not know before this vision of them sitting together that they were good friends while on the earth.

The Boy by the River

After I moved back to Germany in 2005, I became good friends with a woman who was an English student of mine. I had many English students of all ages throughout the entire time we lived in Germany. I taught school and college students ages eight to twenty-five as well as many business professionals. She took classes from me to improve her conversational English for work. We took some nice hikes through the lovely countryside nearby. As we talked, we discovered that we both liked many of the same authors and had some of the same interests. We enjoyed discussing spiritual topics and meditated together a few times. The angels gave me messages and visions for her, although I had not asked. As usual, when the angels gave these to me, they would often pester me until I delivered them. I wrote down all of the messages the angels asked me to give to her. After a few days, I asked if she would like to hear them and she did. She was grateful and moved. She felt that it really helped her move through some obstacles in her life. As we talked over the months, she kept encouraging me to go public with this gift, but I did not feel like I was ready. I also felt that Germany was not ready for someone like me.

Some good friends of hers lost their eight-year-old son to leukemia. Understandably they were having a very difficult time moving beyond their grief. One day she asked me if I could see if their son was all right and in heaven. I had invited them through her to visit me. But understandably they were not comfortable, as they did not know me at all.

Immediately I could see that he was in heaven and he was fine and happy. It was a beautiful summer day. The sun was shining through the lovely green trees, and the weather was perfect. He was riding on a gentle brown horse, and his grandpa was holding the reigns. His grandpa was very loving and patient and was wearing bib overalls. They were walking next to the Kocher River, which was in the valley close to where they lived. The grandpa had fishing poles in his hand. They were both smiling and looked very content. There was a cute brown puppy walking next to the horse. I could see this puppy perfectly but didn't understand its significance. It was such a peaceful and beautiful vision.

What I found especially nice was that when she relayed the message back to the parents, they told her that the boy had liked to fish and had spent time at that river. His grandpa had also loved to fish. I recognized the river, as I had been there myself many times and liked to walk on the serene trails there. Our wedding reception was very near to where I saw them, as it was near to the abbey where we had married. His grandpa had passed away, and I described him well. And the little boy had always wanted a puppy but wasn't allowed to have one while he was living.

I was again impressed with the idea that this child, although he had not had a puppy on the earth and had wanted one, had one in heaven. I loved the fact that he looked so happy and content with his grandpa and that they were both doing something in heaven that they liked to do on the earth.

It was then that I felt I was also made aware that the original earth, in all its splendor, is found in heaven and that this earth we live on is a replica. At this same time, I was given a greater desire to care for and aid in preserving this beautiful earth that we live on.

Love Letters from Heaven

I t was after this year of basking in the light of God and his unconditional love, angelic encounters, and experiences in heaven that this same *knowingness* I had in heaven was present with me most of the time.

I was still trying to keep all of this a secret as much as I could. However, it seemed the angels were guiding people into my life and orchestrating everything. I met new people everywhere I went. Strangers approached me when I was at the hair salon, walking down the street, browsing at the farmer's market, or grocery shopping. Usually they asked, "May I speak with you? I feel like I know you. Are you a healer?" I felt as though I was wearing an invisible sign that read, "Open for Business," one that only their souls could read. They often added, "I don't even know why I am drawn to you, but I feel I need to talk with you."

I was quite used to people telling me their biggest secrets, as this had happened to me my entire life, but this was something entirely different.

I began to know things about people without understanding how. It seemed this same knowingness that I experienced in heaven remained with me. It was as though the angels were reading their hearts and souls and speaking through me. Then I began receiving messages for people close to me. I learned more and more to trust my intuition, as often the messages initially made little sense to me but made complete sense and resonated with the individuals so much that they began to cry. The angels would encourage me, firmly nudge me, and keep me awake at night until I would deliver them. After this happened several times, I finally learned to do as they asked, and I began to write everything down, type it up, and deliver them if the recipient was receptive, as I really wanted my sleep.

What I soon realized was that many of these people had been praying for help or answers to important questions but had not yet learned how to listen. There were many times that the angels wanted me to specifically relay messages to particular people who had been praying for guidance or asking for help in trying to make important decisions.

I also noticed that many people who were drawn to speak with me had loved ones who had passed away and wanted me to deliver a message to them. Often there was some unfinished business or something that they wanted to ask forgiveness for. Many times it was parents who had fallen short of loving their children as they wished they had, and were now in heaven and wanting to ask for forgiveness.

I never had to prepare anything. The messages simply flowed through me. As I stated before, I do not know if this will be my future path or if this part of my life is complete, as this is entirely up to God. I do often still receive messages and pages of messages for people, but it seems to be orchestrated entirely by the angels and not of my choosing.

Usually the angels would *download* around three pages of messages from God, Jesus, guardian angels, guides, and any other help in heaven for me to deliver to the various people I was meeting. I understood—after years of resisting—that this was an incredible privilege. Sometimes these messages did not come immediately but after I prayed and meditated. I often ask for answers if I am looking for guidance or trying to make an important decision. If I don't receive answers to the questions right away, they are usually there right as I wake up the next morning.

These letters were consistently filled with such incredible insight, wisdom, love, hope, and knowledge that it was clear to me that they were *love letters from heaven*. I could never produce such a letter on my own if I tried. Usually the people cried as their souls recognized the messages as the truth. These letters touched them as they were filled with information that I could have never known. Most of the time there were answers to the deepest intimate questions on their hearts. Sometimes they included the encouragement that they needed to pursue their life purposes. Occasionally the messages contained what their soul purpose was. Frequently I would know the names of their angels, guides, or loved ones who had crossed over. Sometimes I could see how many angels they had, what they looked like, if they had male or female energy, and the particular strengths that they carried with them. I often felt as if I had no control over this and the angels were directing everything. In addition, if the angels wanted to get a message to someone, they would pester me until I asked the person if they were interested in receiving messages from their angels or loved ones.

I had learned by now that some angels are much louder than others and therefore easier to hear. Even our guardian angels carry particular attributes to assist us, such as wisdom, perseverance, or strength. These are usually the same things that we need boosts in to fulfill our divine purposes.

After I got used to the whole idea of it and accepted it as a gift, I considered this to be an honor. I had never felt such fulfillment as when the angels were speaking through me. I had known recognition and appreciation in my life before. I had received a lot of recognition in my life for my singing ability. I have sung in front of hundreds of people regularly since I was a teenager and I had especially received a lot of acknowledgment for this God-given talent while I was in Germany. Furthermore, I had consistent recognition in school and work. It was also an honor to be the wife of my husband, who was a well-known and successful businessman in our area. I found tremendous fulfillment in being the mother of Marie. However, working with the angelic realm was fulfillment on a soul level.

I usually spoke with these people at our home. Some of them asked me to teach them how to meditate. I taught anyone who asked. I started teaching a few people in my home what I had learned in heaven. One of them became one of my closest friends in Germany. She called our time together "Karen's School from Heaven."

As Michael earned a very good salary, I never took any payment for delivering these messages or teaching what I had learned in heaven or gained from Mabel. I was usually paid with jars of homemade jelly or jam. We received so much jam over the years that I never had to buy any.

CHAPTER

One Hundred Thousand Angels

Before we moved back to Germany from Shanghai, Marie and I went home for my cousin's wedding in June to Minneapolis. My belief in Mabel as a healer was so strong that I wanted to give this gift of healing to my family. As I had never met anyone like her before, I was certain that my family had not either. I invited her to come home with me to Iowa, and anyone in my family who wished to could have healing sessions with her. Because we are all very close, I wondered if any of them possibly had a similar soul purpose or was as in as much need of healing as I was.

We moved back to Germany at the end of August in 2005. Although I knew our time there was important, I was extremely grateful to leave Shanghai. I was especially thankful when we all returned back to Germany safely and in one piece. I had heard several stories from other Westerners where this was not the case.

It remained a difficult time in many ways. I was still battling the darkness, but this darkness felt different than the one I felt the previous years. It was much more intense. Fortunately now I had the tools to do this, and my spirit was gaining in strength the more time I spent in my spiritual practice. The more I battled, the stronger I grew. It was similar to lifting weights, but I was exercising my spiritual muscles. The more time I spent in prayer and meditation, using this love and light of God, the stronger my connection to heaven and the angels grew.

During this time the angels gave me many physical signs that they were constantly working with me. Besides often having visitations and messages, I kept hearing that I could never ask for too many angels to help me. I repeatedly heard that I could even ask for one hundred thousand angels and that they would come. They assured me that they would always be with me.

One incredibly delightful sign came when a good friend of mine visited me from Australia in the fall of 2005. Her name is also Mary, and her daughter was Marie's best friend in kindergarten and the first grade. She brought a CD with her to share with me that she thought I would like. She had just picked it up while she was traveling in the United Kingdom. It was called *A Hundred Thousand Angels* by Bliss. I loved it immediately, and I found it to be very healing. As I did not have a CD burner at the time, I copied it onto a cassette. Unfortunately I did not copy all of the songs, as I was in a hurry because her visit was brief. I felt kind of disappointed, as I had only copied about three-quarters of the CD. A few months later Michael gave me a new laptop for Christmas with a CD burner built in. I had wanted one for several years. When I used it for the first time, the CD that I had put in to copy was an educational CD. But when I played the first CD I had copied, it was a complete CD of *A Hundred Thousand Angels* by Bliss. How was this possible? The only cassette I had of the original CD was only three-fourths complete and was missing the last three or four songs. I knew it was a gift from the angels, and I thought I could see them giggling with delight. It was a wonderful surprise. By this time I had experienced so many things that I was able to accept this as a gift from them, as unbelievable as it was. I still love this CD. I made several more copies in case the original somehow disappeared. I have shared this CD with several people, and they all found it to be healing.

In telling this story, nowadays it would be very easy to just go on iTunes and download this CD, but this was before the days of iTunes and Amazon in Germany. At this time in 2005, I would have needed to go to the United Kingdom to get the CD. Things similar to this happened quite regularly, and I felt as if they were constantly reminding me that they were with me and that we were protected, despite everything that was going on around us.

Visiting Lourdes

About six months after we moved back to Germany, my sister came to visit us. A few months before this, she asked me if Marie and I would like to accompany her to Lourdes in France. She had just left the convent and was going to begin her life as a doctor of infectious diseases again. I could still feel intense darkness around us, but this darkness was different and stronger than the previous evil I felt years earlier. Although my physical symptoms were gone, Marie still often had a fever and bronchitis. She also verbalized feeling this evil and often had trouble falling asleep and would wake up with frightful nightmares filled with ghosts and witches. She would describe these dreams perfectly and how they were chasing her. Therefore, I felt a very strong calling to accept my sister's invitation.

I feel very fortunate because I have had the opportunity to visit many wonderful places in the last twenty years. As Michael enjoyed traveling and also loved to drive long distances very quickly, I was able to visit many countries and see many beautiful cities. However, of all the cities I have ever been to, Lourdes struck me as the most joy-filled. I have also never seen so many angels on earth in my entire life as I saw there.

It is seated at the foothills of the Pyrenees Mountains in Southern France and is one of the most famous shrines for Roman Catholics, attracting more than a million pilgrims each year. There have been thousands of miraculous cures of many diseases at the shrine regardless of religious affiliation.

In 1858, in the grotto of Massabielle near Lourdes, a beautiful lady appeared eighteen times to Bernadette Soubirous, a fourteen-year-old peasant girl. She identified herself as the "Immaculate Conception." She gave Bernadette this message for all: "Pray and do penance for the conversion of the whole world." This beautiful lady is believed to have been the blessed Mother, Mary.

During the ninth apparition Bernadette was directed to a spring that had not previously existed in the grotto. Hundreds witnessed as Bernadette followed the direction of the Blessed Virgin and dug with her hand in the dirt, discovering the spring. The water flowing from this spring was eventually declared miraculous, healing the sick and the lame. It was estimated that more than four thousand miraculous healings occurred during the first fifty years alone, and thousands have been healed since that time by consuming this water or bathing in the water that wells out of the grotto. Bernadette was canonized a saint in 1933.

While we were traveling through France, I was thankful that my sister spoke French fluently, as I did not. Upon our arrival, what struck me the most, besides the immediate joy that I felt, was that I could see angels everywhere. I saw angels of all sizes accompanying the people walking on the street. I had never seen so many angels in one place on the earth. Nor had I ever seen angels before that looked like they were twenty feet tall. What I noticed was how joyful the people all looked. While there, I saw many people pushing others in wheelchairs or carrying stretchers with pilgrims who were too ill to walk. Everyone looked so joyful. I feel it was greatly because of the presence of so many angels.

I believe that this trip to Lourdes was instrumental in sustaining and protecting us through the most difficult and darkest times that were still ahead of us. I am still grateful to my sister for asking us to take this trip with her. I feel that she was divinely inspired.

Marie's symptoms did lessen after she bathed in the healing water in Lourdes, but they worsened again a few months later. She had bronchitis so often that the doctors told me that she would be acquiring scar tissue on her bronchia and would very soon have asthma. I saw plenty of children in Asia with asthma, and I didn't want this for Marie. I started praying and asking for direction to help me find someone who could find the root cause of her continued sickness. I then met a key friend in my life who helped me in many ways. Her name is Dorothea.

Meeting Dorothea

Now that I was back in Germany, I began singing with my choir again. Although I felt that I needed some recovery time from all of the things that I had recently experienced and engaged slowly, singing has always been healing for me, and I missed my friends. At this same time, I was asked to help out a local choir that needed a soloist for their annual festival. They asked me to sing "Amazing Grace" as well as "Oh, Happy Day" with them. This invitation proved to be a blessing to me in many ways.

First of all I met a nice new group of people and had the opportunity to sing with them at many occasions during the subsequent years. In addition, I found a wonderful new life-long friend. Through this new friend I met one of the most influential people in my life that taught and assisted me with healing through the following years.

I immediately liked the people in the choir. They were very nice and welcoming, and the first rehearsal went very well, as if we had sung together a long time. During the singing break I was drawn to a woman named Dorothea. I felt like I definitely knew her, and she felt the same. I had never had this strong feeling before except for when I met Michael. I asked her if she had worked at any of the places that Michael or I had worked. I wondered if we had previously taken classes together, gone to the same church, or sung in the same choir. She wondered the same things. We could not think of anywhere we might have met before. We conversed more in the following rehearsals. Eventually she invited me to her home, and it developed into a close friendship.

I soon discovered that her faith in God was strong and she had experienced much grief and trial in her life. She had one wonderfully brilliant son who was in high school but had miscarried several other children. Some of them were lost during childbirth. She was still in the process of grieving. I could tell that she had a strong love for God. I marveled at her strength and how kind and giving she was despite all that she had been through. I believe I have only met one other person in my life who has a heart as big and soft as Dorothea's and who has a love for all children and living creatures as great as hers. This person was my roommate and best friend throughout college. I later learned that she was also highly sensitive to energy like me and very intuitive, and her prayers were very powerful.

Although I had a few close friends I could share some of my spiritual experiences of the previous years with, I still felt that I needed to hide this part of myself regarding what I had experienced in heaven and with the angels from most people. I am very close with my sisters and brothers and was able to share some things with them, but they lived four thousand miles away. Thankfully with Dorothea, I was completely free to be myself—angels, heaven, and all. She is the only one I could share everything with regarding all that I had experienced during the previous years. She completely believed in me, and I will be forever grateful that I had this one person in my life I could confide in and share this part of myself that I otherwise felt I needed to hide.

She was eager to learn everything that I could teach her and was always very gracious. But what she could not see was how much she was helping me and teaching me simultaneously. I believe that she saved me in many ways by allowing me to be my true and authentic self all the while we were together. She consistently encouraged me and reminded me that I had these gifts, especially when I needed it the most. Her faith in me continually reminded me to have faith in myself and in turn in God, especially when someone close to me began to beat me down further as I rose up and grew stronger.

As our friendship developed, she told me about a healer who had helped her tremendously. She had heard about him from another woman from a nearby town. This woman had terminal cancer and was sent home from the hospital to die. Before she left the hospital to go home for what would be her final days on the earth, a woman she had never seen before entered her hospital room and gave her a healer's number and encouraged her to call him. She called this man and began working with him. Now more than twelve years later she is still alive. She attributed her complete healing to this man. His name is Herr Weng.

The Energy Healer

I strongly felt that I should bring Marie to this healing practitioner to get at the root cause of her bronchitis, as traditional medicine was not helping. Around this same time Michael had developed severe pain in his back that ran down his leg. His pain was so extreme that he could sometimes hardly stand or walk. As he often needed to stand long hours at trade shows and sit in planes for many hours, he was in pain much of the time. He went through the proper medical tests, and it was determined that he had a slipped disk and needed to have back surgery. I convinced him to see Herr Weng before he committed to surgery. I do not think he would have agreed to see him had his pain not have been so severe and if he did not dislike hospitals so much. He had never been ill before in his life and did not appreciate his first experiences of having an MRI and other medical tests.

Together we traveled to meet Herr Weng two and a half hours away near Ulm in Bavaria. He specialized in homeopathy and kinesiology. I liked him immediately. I believe he is possibly the holiest and most humble man I have ever met. Although he is compact in stature, I had never felt so much strength and power originating from a human being before. It reminded me of the power I felt in the presence of Archangel Raphael. I immediately recognized this as the power of God.

Amazingly, he put his hands on Michael's lower back for what seemed like two seconds and Michael's pain was gone. We both found this to be incredible. Now he did not need surgery. Michael was thrilled and asked him where he had learned to do this, and he told him that what he practices is centuries old. Michael was extremely impressed and asked him why everyone did not know about this type of alternative therapy called energy healing.

When I had my first session with him, the first thing he told me was that he saw that I was using much of my own energy to try to heal others. This left me drained of my own energy and abnormally hungry. He asked me to always imagine the healing power and the light of God going directly from God to the person I was sending healing energy to. I should not imagine the light of God going through me and then to the person. He was right! I had been doing this. I was impressed that he knew this without me saying a word, and I was thankful that he understood me so well. Sometimes it is so good just to be seen or understood, even if it is from one person. From that day on I changed my approach back to the way I was originally taught by Mabel and the angels.

Honestly when my first healing session with him was finished, I wondered, *Is that it?* He was very kind and humble and said very few words. I did not immediately understand the power in the words he was speaking or the intention he was setting while working with me. He sent us home with some homeopathic medicine to take to build up Marie's immune system and some phrases to say every day.

That evening it hit me. It felt like the difference between night and day. I felt immediate release, peace, and renewed strength and energy, and I slept wonderfully. It was as if any fear or darkness was immediately washed away. Although I had witnessed the gifts he possessed when he immediately healed Michael's back, it was only weeks later that I recognized his gifts of acute intuition and the power of the phrases he had spoken and had asked me to repeat twice daily.

As the original phrases were in German, I have translated them as best as I can. They were as follows: "Thank you, God, that all negative energy by me is now dissolved. Thank you, God, that I have a new connection to your divine energy. Thank you, God, that Marie's bronchitis is now dissolved to the root cause and her health is in your divine order. Thank you, God, that Marie has a new connection to your divine energy."

After we met with him once or twice, an energetic connection was established, and then it was possible to speak with him over the phone if we needed further homeopathic or energetic assistance.

Marie's immune system began to improve almost immediately. She rarely had bronchitis from then on and seldom missed school. From that time on when she has gotten sick, she has been able to recover on her own. I knew that I did not have to worry about her getting asthma anymore.

As I previously mentioned, I did not initially recognize the power in the phrases he asked me to say every day, but I did notice immediately the results and the restoration of my energy and peace after meeting with him.

As the darkness over our family persisted and intensified in the following years and I was not certain why or where it was coming from, I went to see him a few more times and asked him to teach me his main principles of healing. Again I was following my intuition and felt a very strong nudging to meet with him and learn what I could. He agreed to teach me and told me that he had taught many others who had then opened their own healing centers. He also knew where the source of this evil was coming from.

What I did not know until I went for my first teaching lesson with him was that he was using the light and the pure, powerful, infinite healing energy of God to heal. This was exactly how he said it, which was exactly how I knew it from heaven. How he worked was almost exactly the way that Mabel and the angels had taught me, and I knew it was divine intervention. There were a few important things he taught me that made a great difference, and I felt as though these made what I was practicing more complete.

As I mentioned, I was incorrectly trying to harness the light of God and then send this to others to heal them. He told me to always imagine the light going directly from God to myself or whomever I was praying for or sending healing energy to. This was how the angels taught me, but somehow I had started visualizing the light going from God to me to the person, and that was detrimental to me, as it drained my energy and was not as effective for the person receiving the healing.

He advised me to imagine the healing light of God filled with the pure, powerful, infinite, and unconditional love of God. Then I should imagine this light completely surrounding myself or the person I am hoping to help heal. The person should be in this pillar or cylinder of light, which was coming directly from God onto him or her. The cylinder should be about as big around as the person with his or her arms stretched out. Then I imagine this healing light of God permeating every cell of the individual's body and washing away any negativity, fear, and pain, which then drains into the ground afterward. Then I say, "Thank you, God, that all negative energy by me is now dissolved. Thank you, God that I have a new connection to your divine energy." I then should spend time visualizing this powerful light and energy of God washing over me and filling every cell of my body, rejuvenating, and healing me or whoever I was sending healing energy to.

He explained that another way to imagine God was as an infinite gas tank with an infinite supply of his divine love and energy being pumped to each individual person I wanted to send healing energy to.

It was important that each person had an individual connection to God. In other words, each person should be in his or her very own cylinder of light or have his or her own gas pump/hose that is connected to the infinite source of God's divine energy. No two people should share a connection.

I think I could possibly write a book about all of the countless ways that Herr Weng helped me, and what he taught me during the following five years. He was a tremendous blessing and genuinely helped us to survive the most horrific times. Most importantly he taught me to use this healing light twice a day to energetically protect my husband, my daughter, and myself from this darkness.

It was now 2006, and I thought at that time that we were over the worst of times. I am glad that I didn't know that my greatest trial, disappointment, loss, and betrayal were all still in front of me. I would need everything I had learned and every ounce of faith to make it through the years that would follow. What I learned in heaven would serve as a lamp that lit my way through and out of the darkest and most difficult times that were to come. I also could not have imagined where this new, more intense dark energy was coming from. What was most important was that I now had the sharpened tools that I needed and a few key people in my life to help me through the upcoming battle of the next six years.

As I mentioned earlier, upon receiving these teachings in heaven, some of it did not initially make sense to me, or I did not see the first years how it applied to me, or my life, until later when it all became evident. I feel that what I learned in heaven literally saved my life and the lives of my family. Now I hope this information can help and heal others as it has helped me.

Afterword

I believe my story is one that affirms that the human spirit prevails! No matter how broken in spirit you have felt, no matter how you have failed, no matter the amount of darkness that has persisted against you in your own life, all of heaven is waiting for you to ask for help! I encourage you to take the time to connect with heaven and listen to your own inner voice. Each of us has much more love in heaven than we can begin to imagine, watching over us, rooting for us, and cheering us on!

My greatest desire is that anyone reading this book will feel closer to our heavenly Father and have a deeper knowing and understanding of who they truly are through his love and mercy for them. One of the greatest impressions I was left with after every journey to heaven is that God wants us to know that every one of us as his children are unconditionally loved, powerful, and magnificent, as we are an extension of him and he truly lives in us. We are all *one* with him and therefore, united with one another. In addition, that God longs for every single soul to return home to him.

I do believe there must be others like me who have had similar experiences and are possibly afraid to speak about them as I was. As we are in need of hope while we are on this harsh earth, I believe more people will be having heavenly and angelic experiences and will be coming forward with their stories. *Now* is the time to bring as much love and light as possible into this world. Every single person is more powerful than they possibly realize and can make a tremendous difference!

The Hundred Things I
Learned in Heaven

I believe that I learned much more than one hundred things. I have included here what I feel may be the most important things.

1. God is the Creator of the universe and the only Creator in the universe.

2. God is our heavenly Father.

3. God loves each of his children the same. His love for each of us is pure, powerful, unconditional, and infinite.

4. The light and the love of God are the most powerful weapons and tools in the entire universe. No amount of darkness is as powerful as the love and light of God.

5. As we are his children, we are all extensions of him and are created in his light and in his image. We are so much a part of him that he exists in every cell of our body and in our DNA. Therefore, we all carry his same power, creative energy, and love inside of us. His love is constant, merciful, and much more inclusive than I ever imagined.

6. God's love and mercy for us is so great that he wants each of his children to return to their true home in heaven not because we have done something to deserve it but because of his great mercy and what he has done for us.

7. I understood that I had not earned God's love for me. Nor could I do anything to deserve it or to change it. This is God's love for every one of us, each of his creations.

8. God said to me, "Many of my children do not accept me or acknowledge me as their Father, but still my love and mercy for them remains."

9. Ascending to heaven felt like I was being carried quickly but gently straight up toward the sun. It was effortless, and it felt natural like I had done this many times before.

10. At first as I was ascending quickly upward, the light was golden yellow like the sun, and then the light changed to pure bright white the closer I got. Even though my eyes were closed, I instinctively raised my arms to shield them, thinking I might be blinded as the light became more and more intense.

11. The joy that I felt was so overwhelming as I ascended that I could not help but laugh out loud with euphoric elation.

12. There are no human words to describe the love of God. The only way I could begin to come close to describing the unconditional love of God that I felt every time while I was ascending to and in heaven would be if I took all of the love I had for everyone I loved in this lifetime and then multiplied that by an infinite number. This is also inadequate, as the love I felt had no limits and had no bounds.

13. The closest way I could describe the complete joy that I felt while I was ascending to and in heaven would be if I took the most joyful moments of my entire life and the most intimate moments of bliss and oneness that I had ever experienced with my husband and then multiplied that by an infinite number.

14. Every time I was in heaven, I was bursting with feelings of joy, happiness, complete fulfillment, safety, and belonging.

15. We are all much more connected than I ever realized, and in truth we are *one* with God and therefore with one another.

16. Heaven is our true home.

17. God and our angels know us from the beginning of the creation of our souls. My soul—and I believe all of our souls—are much older than I ever imagined.

18. Every soul, upon entering heaven, is warmly welcomed by at least one person and usually a group of people who love them. Every soul is escorted to heaven by at least one angel.

19. No matter how much we feel we may have failed in our lives, God wants us to see ourselves through his eyes. In his eyes we are pure, innocent, and completely and unconditionally loved just as we are.

20. I observed my dad's welcome party after he entered heaven, and it was individualized to fit what would bring him the most joy, fun, and happiness.

21. The first time I met three of my angels, they were completely delighted to see me. It was as if we knew one another forever. They were thrilled that I asked them for help. They encouraged me to ask for help in every circumstance. It did not matter how great or how small my need was or how often I asked. They told me to "ask, ask, ask!"

22. Our angels love us with the same unconditional love of God. In their eyes we are perfect, whole, and complete just as we are. Although they knew all of my faults and weaknesses, it all did not matter as there was no judgment.

23. God and our angels treasure everything about us. They asked me to try to love myself as they loved me now that I could see myself through God's eyes.

24. All communication in heaven and in the realms between heaven and earth was telepathic—thought-to-thought, feeling-to-feeling, and soul-to-soul communion. It was natural and easy. There was no room for miscommunication this way.

25. One of the greatest gifts we can offer our heavenly Father is healthy self-love and self-care. Loving, honoring, forgiving, and accepting ourselves is one of the greatest gifts we can give to God, as we are in truth *one* with him, and this returns love, honor, forgiveness, and acceptance back to him.

26. God, Jesus, Mary, and the angels and saints in heaven hear our prayers every time we pray. Heaven is just waiting for us to ask, and they are constantly watching over us and speaking to us. Because man has been given free will on the earth, they cannot intervene except in some life-threatening situations unless we ask.

27. We should ask for help in all circumstances by praying. Trust that our prayers have been heard. Surrender the situation to them.

Listen for answers and steps to take through quiet meditation. Take action and begin with small steps.

28. When I saw God for the first time, he looked like a big oval-shaped white cloud of pure glory, and I felt an overwhelming unconditional *fatherly* love.

29. I felt that God wanted me to see my true magnificence. I saw myself for the first time as he saw me, and I was a million times more significant than I ever imagined. I understood that this is how he saw every one of his children.

30. I saw many indescribably beautiful things in heaven that completely defied all logic and natural laws on the earth.

31. God and I sat down together in heaven to plan the life that I am living now. He asked me what I wanted to do and where I wanted to go.

32. This immense unconditional love is what God feels for every one of his children regardless of whether they accept him as their Father or not.

33. God is omnipresent, which means that he exists everywhere and is in every cell of our bodies and even our DNA. Therefore, we all have access to his pure, powerful, infinite, unconditional love and divine creative energy at all times if we remain close to him.

34. Without God I am nothing. But when I remain close to him and stay in relationship with him, I am never without him. And therefore, I am never without his power, infinite love, mercy, grace, and abundant blessings.

35. God impressed upon my heart his desperate longing for each and every one of his children to return home to him.

36. I chose everything I experienced in this lifetime. Therefore, the one I need to forgive the most is myself. Furthermore, because every person is connected and *one* in truth, the one I need to forgive the most is myself.

37. I chose everything in this lifetime to help me reach my divine purpose.

38. I had a much bigger role than I had previously realized in planning my lifetime. I chose together with God, my angels,

and spirit guides the major soul lessons and people in my life, the triumphs as well as trials.

39. I was given an *understanding* in these realms and a *knowing* that I had never experienced before. I suddenly knew things without knowing how I knew them.

40. There needs to be a balance between giving and receiving. It needs to flow in a circle.

41. Our life on earth is a gift that is meant to be enjoyed within God's will.

42. In heaven it is only possible to experience love, joy, peace, hope, and all other positive emotions. On earth, because man is given free will, we have the opportunity to experience all of the contrasting emotions, such as fear, hate, despair, and sorrow. It is not possible to learn about pain or fear from a textbook or teacher in heaven.

43. I saw how everything and everyone is part of one another and how it all fits together like a perfectly designed jigsaw puzzle. Everything is divinely orchestrated.

44. There is purpose in everything that happens, and there are no coincidences.

45. There is a much greater order and a bigger plan for everything in the universe than I could have ever contemplated.

46. I was limiting God with my own limiting beliefs about myself and about God. God had much greater plans for me than I had ever imagined for myself.

47. Our souls are eternal. This life I am living is like one grain of sand on a vast beach, one drop of water in a boundless ocean, or one small section of a beautiful never-ending tapestry. Our souls are really in a miraculous cycle of life, death, and rebirth. Our souls never die. They only evolve.

48. From my soul's perspective the traumas I have experienced in this lifetime are like small slits in the fabric of a never-ending tapestry. These small slits have very little significance in the big scheme of things.

49. Any suffering I have experienced was all being used for something good and was all for my highest good. All suffering and literally

every teardrop is saved and transmuted into something great and useful.

50. The traumas that I experienced provided my soul with excellent opportunities to learn lessons that I might not otherwise has learned, and they caused my soul to grow and expand.

51. Every traumatic event that happened in my life was for my highest good. Things that are for our highest good are all of the events, lessons, and trials that we go through in our lives that keep us on our paths to our soul purposes. Often these things do not feel like they are good for us at all, but they are exactly what we need or have chosen.

52. It is a tremendous privilege to come to the earth for the opportunity of learning lessons and for the expansion and evolution of our souls. I was shown a line with what looked like thousands of people lined up, wanting to return to earth for this opportunity.

53. Love is the highest vibrating emotion of all. Fear is the lowest.

54. At any given time in our lives we have either chosen to move toward love or toward fear with our thoughts, what we say, and our actions. I am much more responsible for the outcome of my life than I realized.

55. We all come to the earth with our own individual curriculum. It is similar to attending school or college. We all have specific lessons that we want to learn.

56. Everything is already planned ahead of time as far as people and teachers coming into our lives. However, much of the outcome can be created by us with our thoughts and actions and is more similar to being sketched in pencil rather than written in stone.

57. Sometimes the greatest teachers in my life were the same people who caused me the most emotional hurt or harm. These events were an opportunity that provided me with important lessons on forgiveness, trust, love, perseverance, faith, self-acceptance, and patience.

58. I was in a monumental museum in heaven, where all of the most important books, inventions, scrolls, and works of art since the beginning of mankind were kept. The guide, who was an angel, told me that these were all of the original creations since the

beginning of mankind on the earth. The ones on the earth were replicas.

59. My body in heaven was limitless. I was often floating or flying slightly above the ground. Or I just had to think about where I wanted to go, and I was there instantaneously.

60. I saw many things that defied the natural laws on the earth, such as a sunset under the ground, a table that had many types and shades of wood within one cross section of a tree, flowers and vines growing out of stone, a small diamond on the end of every blade of grass, buildings made out of large crystals, and the grass dancing with the horses, etc.

61. The colors in heaven are vibrant and alive, and I saw colors I have never seen before on the earth. I compare it to the movie *The Wizard of Oz* because the movie begins in black-and-white, and then when they arrive in Oz, it changes into bursting, vibrant Technicolor. This is similar to comparing the colors on earth to those in heaven.

62. In heaven there consistently seemed to be anything and everything that one could imagine to bring enjoyment within God's will. It was as though I just had to think of something or someone, and either I was transported to that place or the person or thing instantly appeared before me.

63. The altar of God appeared as though it was made out of white marble, and the room it was in was grand and majestic. There I saw God and Jesus standing on a large altar. This was the only time I saw God as a man. He appeared as an older man with a white beard, similar to how he is depicted in the famous fresco by Michelangelo found in the Sistine Chapel. He did not look frail or weak but fit and lively. They were all honoring the queen of heaven, the blessed Mother, Mary. I was completely enamored by her presence. She radiated pure motherly love, strength, peace, hope, and joy. Beyond them was row upon row upon row of angels as high up as I could see. I knew that it was a never-ending tower of angels.

64. I visited many times a spectacular city. Everything about it was impressive and amazing. It was shining like diamonds or crystals

from a distance. I was inside many buildings. Most of them were round in shape with high ceilings covered with jewels of all different colors and varieties. Some of the buildings looked as though they were carved out of a very large amethyst crystal. There was an abundance of every kind of precious metals and jewels in the buildings of this city, and the walkways were made out of raw gold.

65. God never asked me to be perfect, follow all the rules perfectly, or sacrifice my life completely for anyone. After I reviewed several of my lifetimes, he said to me, "My dear one, you completely missed the point! I never asked you to be perfect or to deny yourself or your feelings. I never asked you to be a sacrifice. I never asked you for any of these things. Your life on earth was a gift to be enjoyed. What I wanted was for you to be happy. What I wanted was for you to understand and remember who you are through me and to live your most authentic and joyful life possibly through me!"

66. Healthy self care and self love are two of the greatest gifts that I can give back to God.

67. I was shown by the angels myself in my highest form and in my true power as they saw me. I was twenty feet tall, bright white, and magnificent.

68. God asked me to choose happiness instead of sacrifice. I do not need to sacrifice my life for others. The one true sacrifice has already been completed by Jesus, and I cannot add to this sacrifice or diminish it in any way. It is perfect, whole, and complete.

69. God the Father is like the sun. He is immense, glorious, and bright! He provides light and warmth to everything he touches. He sustains all life. He does not discriminate. He is constant. He never changes. We as his children are like the rays of the sun. We are all extensions of him and remain 100 percent pure sun, even if we feel like we are millions of miles away from our source.

70. There are children and pets in heaven.

71. Every angel I ever met, whether a powerful archangel or one of my guardian angels, always made it known to me how much they loved me from the beginning of time. Every single one was

familiar and it felt as though we had always been close friends. I knew that they knew and loved everything about me and did not judge my faults, although I knew that they were aware of them.

72. I have seen several times people performing jobs in heaven. It appeared as though every person had his or her dream job as they were all joyful and celebrating.

73. We each have a highest self. This is the part of us that remains close to God in heaven and remembers our true identity as a magnificent, powerful, child of God. This highest self also retains the knowledge of past lives and the important lessons learned. This self also knows the lessons we are currently working on.

74. We all have access at any time to the wisdom of our souls, which retains the knowledge learned throughout every lifetime ever lived. Access can be gained through prayer and meditation.

75. God and the angels asked me to let go of my limiting beliefs. These are beliefs that we hold either consciously or subconsciously that do not serve us in a positive way. They act as obstacles to manifesting and attracting what we want. Some of mine were as follows: *If I am not perfect, then I am not worthy of love or acceptance. I am not good enough because I am damaged.* God asked me to release these beliefs because they were limiting how he could work through me. God does not want us to limit him and how he can work through us. God has much bigger plans for us than we often have for ourselves.

76. When we confess our sins to God, they truly are forgiven and remembered no more.

77. There is a real battle for every soul in the spiritual realms.

78. I experienced in a most profound way God's deep sadness for any of his children who are lost or do not know him. He loves all of his children the same whether they accept him or not. He created every soul and truly knows them by heart, loves them unconditionally, and calls them each by name. He has counted every hair on their heads and treasures every one of them.

79. God told me that many of his children cannot comprehend his love for them. He said, "I am their Father in heaven who

desperately wants to bless each of them with more goodness than they can possibly imagine."

80. It was revealed to me that for many people it is very difficult to believe that they have a Father in heaven who loves them this much and is this merciful because they never had a loving father while on the earth.

81. Everyone is born with everything they need to complete their missions or soul purposes. Everyone has a soul purpose and every purpose is important!

82. What is important when our souls depart from this earth plain and our physical bodies die is that we accept God as our heavenly Father or Jesus as his Son. As God, Jesus, and the Holy Spirit are all separate and yet one that cannot be separated, if you accept the one true God, you accept his Son and vice versa.

83. All of heaven rejoices every time a soul enters heaven. Every soul entering heaven is considered an equal victory.

84. Everything in the universe is composed of energy and is vibrating. The speed at which something is vibrating is called the frequency.

85. God is the highest vibrating being in the universe. Angels' frequencies are very high, and they have the ability to go between God and men, who are vibrating on a lower level. Some people have raised their vibration enough to communicate with God and angels. Everyone has the ability to communicate with angels and to hear God's voice. The best way to raise our vibration is through consistent prayer and deep meditation, keeping our thoughts and emotions positive, praising God, and doing things that bring us joy.

86. Never underestimate the power of just one person in prayer.

87. We all have a dark and light side. The angels asked me to stop fearing my dark side and to accept and embrace it, as whatever I focus on will expand and therefore be strengthened. Embracing it does not mean submitting to it. If I embrace it with the powerful love of God, knowing that this love conquers all fear, I strengthen my light side.

88. As humans, we all have shadow sides, and we all will be tempted. Giving in to temptation is what we call sin.

89. Just because God bestows us his infinite mercy does not mean that we are free to sin. There are always consequences for every thought and every action, as there are many universal and spiritual laws in place.

90. There are six main ways that sin affects us. Sin places a barrier between God and ourselves so that his blessings cannot reach us. It causes our hearts to harden, and then we are unable to receive the blessings of our divine destiny. Sin lowers our vibration and makes it difficult to hear our intuition or the voice of God. The more we sin, the more layers or what look like hard shells of negative energy are placed around our hearts. Sin often hurts those we love and then returns like a boomerang to hurt us. Sin often causes guilt and shame that ultimately harm us, and it can affect our eternal destiny.

91. With every thought or action, we are moving toward love or toward fear.

92. Just as prayer and meditation raise our vibration and cause things of a higher vibration to be drawn to us, sin lowers our vibration and draws negative people and events into our lives.

93. God does not want us to suffer, and he is never the reason for our suffering. Only good things can transpire from God. However, he allows these universal laws to exist, as well as the darkness. These things exist for our soul's expansion and evolution while on the earth.

94. For every thought we think and every action we take, we will attract a force with an equal frequency.

95. Choosing to have such a strong relationship with God so that we choose not to sin because we know that it does not honor him and does not honor ourselves would please God the most. His greatest hope is that we understand his love for us and desire a close relationship with him.

96. God wants each of us to experience an abundance of love, happiness, health, wealth, and much more goodness than we can begin to imagine while we are on the earth. This includes whatever our hearts' desires are. An abundance of everything is already waiting for us in heaven. This is similar to a huge

warehouse of presents ready to be sent by express mail to us and opened. It is our divine destiny as the children of the Most High King.

97. God would most prefer that no man be ashamed to call him God, Father, Papa, Daddy, or whatever name is most familiar and affectionate for you.

98. From what I experienced thousands of times, every soul had an opportunity to accept or acknowledge God as their Father or Jesus as their Savior even after they died. If they sincerely repented and accepted God or Jesus, they were always accepted back into heaven.

99. All of the people I met in heaven always wish the people they love on the earth love and happiness. Often they had an increased awareness of how they had hurt someone on the earth and wished to apologize.

100. Numerous times I saw that what we individually experience in heaven is what brings us the most joy. I saw many times that we have some ability to create in heaven whatever brings us the most joy and happiness—of course, that is within God's will.

Learning to Meditate Mabel's Way

Here is how Mabel taught me to meditate. It is rather simple. I still meditate this way to this day, but I incorporate things that I learned from Herr Weng in my daily practice now. I will explain all of this in the following section.

First light a white candle. Ask for the white light of God to protect you. Begin with a simple prayer and invite God, Jesus, the Holy Spirit, your angels, and the archangels Michael (protection), Raphael (healing), Gabriel (communication), and Uriel (forgiveness) to be with you (and whatever other heavenly being you feel close to). Thank them for being with you and protecting you.

Mabel meditates in a lotus position. I found this to be difficult, so she taught me the next best position. Sit on a chair with your back straight and head held up as if you are balancing a book on top of your head. Feet should be flat on the floor. Hands are palms down and resting on the thighs above the knees.

Close your eyes and imagine a strong, thick chord of light coming directly from God in heaven through the top of your head (where the soft spot is on a baby). Know that you are then connected to heaven. Imagine this chord attaching to your hips and into the center of the earth. This is your grounding chord.

Now focus on the love and light of God. Feel and imagine as much love as you can imagine. Continue to breath. Imagine the light as sunshine coming through the clouds. Just continue to breath and focus on God's love and light. Muster up as many feelings of love as you can. If you do not yet have a strong love for God, then first think about the love you have for someone else. Set a timer for ten minutes. At the end of the ten minutes when you are in this space and have raised your vibration by focusing on

God's love, that is the best time to ask a question, receive an answer, or ask a prayer request.

Say a closing prayer, thanking all of them for being with you. Whatever is in your heart is fine.

She advised me to do this for at least ten minutes twice a day. She also taught me to expand this light to fill the room you are in, your entire home, and the neighborhood, and then you could expand it and send it out to the entire world.

This same light and love is what she taught me to send to anyone I would like to send healing energy to. Or I could send it to my own body if I had pain or felt any negative energy.

Thank God and the others from heaven for being with you.

Do not be concerned if you begin to sway back and forth. This often happens when you are really connected to heaven.

My Spiritual Practice Today

Here is my daily practice today and how I have combined what I learned from Herr Weng and Mabel and the angels. This explanation may seem long, but once you practice it for a while, it only takes a few minutes every day in addition to the time you would like to meditate. I try to meditate when I begin my day and in the early evening.

Get in the meditation pose—feet flat on the floor, back straight, hands palms down on the thighs above the knees. Imagine a thick rope of light coming directly from God in heaven through the top of your head. This rope connects to your hips and is securely fastened to the center of the earth. Because I need extra grounding, I make this rope as wide as my hips.

I begin by saying the Our Father. I thank God, Jesus, the Holy Spirit, Mary, the archangels, and my angels for being with me. I especially ask Archangel Michael to protect me every time I do my spiritual practice and throughout each day and evening. His light is purplish blue. I spend a minute or two thanking and praising God. This opens up the heavens.

Then I concentrate on the light and the love of God. I imagine the light of God coming directly from heaven as a cylinder of light that surrounds me. This light is as big around as my body with my arms stretched to both sides. This light is filled with God's pure, powerful, infinite, and unconditional love. It is also filled with his power, divine wisdom, healing energy, and joy. I imagine this light washing over me and permeating every cell of my body.

I imagine this light washing away any fear, pain, depression, and negative energy, and then it goes into the earth, where the angels are waiting to take it away and transmute it. Then I say, "Thank you, God, that all negative energy by me is now dissolved."

Here is where I also sometimes add if necessary, "Thank you, God, that all bonds of negative energy (psychic chords) between me and [insert name] are now dissolved." We have psychic or etheric chords with everyone we have relationships with, and we exchange energy through these. If the chords are healthy, they are light pink. If they are unhealthy, they look brown or black. Sometimes if the chords or bonds are thick or toxic, I ask St. Michael to come with his sword of white light and help me to cut them. We only sever what is negative. The love always remains.

Then after I focus on this love for a while and muster up as much love as I possibly can, I then say the words, "Thank you, God, that I have a new connection to your infinite love and divine energy."

I say my prayer request then. "Thank you, God, that everything with [insert name or situation] is in your divine order, and it is healed to the root cause." The example I use in the book is as follows: "Thank you, God, that Marie's bronchitis is healed to the root cause and her health is in your divine order."

This same procedure is what I use if I am requested to send healing energy to someone else. The more time you spend focusing on the love and light of God washing over the person, the more powerful it is. In addition, the more time you spend practicing using the light of God, the more powerful the healing energy becomes.

Then I spend more time focusing on this love and light and *feeling* the love and light. After I focus on God's love and light for a minimum of ten minutes, I listen for answers and messages. When finished, I say a short prayer and thank all of them for being with me and guiding me.

Of course, there are some days that I praise him much longer or spend much more time sending someone the healing love and light of God, but this is the basic practice that I follow.

About the Author

Karen Bauer was born in Iowa and was raised on a large farm with her parents and eight brothers and sisters. She graduated from Iowa State University with a B.S. in Food and Nutrition/Dietetics and a minor in Hotel and Restaurant Management. She worked as a Registered Dietitian and teacher in Minneapolis, MN before marrying her German husband.

After marrying, she moved to Germany. She worked in the corporate world, taught English lessons, and continued her hobby as a musician. Her husbands' job caused them to also reside in Singapore, Japan, and China. Throughout their twenty-two years together, she had the opportunity of meeting people from many countries and learning about their cultures and beliefs.

She became ill after the birth of their daughter in Singapore in 1996 and experienced many frightening events. After six years of illness where no medical tests revealed a diagnosis, she sought help from a spiritual healer and hypnotherapist from Hong Kong. In these healing sessions, Karen was taken multiple times to heaven for learning and healing and emerged from these sessions completely healed of her symptoms.

After returning to Germany, she began to share these truths and the newly acquired gifts she received while in heaven. She now feels called to share the hundred life-changing truths that she learned while in heaven from God and the angels in the form of this book.

Karen currently lives near Minneapolis, MN, with her daughter and is an author, healer, teacher, dietitian, and musician.

Made in the USA
Lexington, KY
11 March 2019